Your
Horoscope
2023

....

Libra

24 September – 23 October

igloobooks

igloobooks

Published in 2022
First published in the UK by Igloo Books Ltd
An imprint of Igloo Books Ltd
Cottage Farm, NN6 0BJ, UK
Owned by Bonnier Books
Sveavägen 56, Stockholm, Sweden
www.igloobooks.com

Copyright © 2022 Igloo Books Ltd

0722 001
2 4 6 8 10 9 7 5 3 1
ISBN 978-1-80108-403-1

Written by Sally Kirkman
Additional content by Belinda Campbell and Denise Evans

Cover designed by Richard Sykes
Interiors designed by Chris Stanley
Edited by Luke Robertson

Printed and manufactured in China

CONTENTS

. . . .

INTRODUCTION
. . . .

This 15-month guide has been designed and written to give a concise and accessible insight into both the nature of your star sign and the year ahead. Divided into two main sections, the first part of this guide will give you an overview of your character in order to help you understand how you think, perceive the world and interact with others and – perhaps just as importantly – why. You'll soon see that your zodiac sign is not just affected by a few stars in the sky, but by planets, elements and a whole host of other factors, too.

The second part of this guide is made up of daily forecasts. Use these to increase your awareness of what might appear on your horizon so that you're better equipped to deal with the days ahead. While this should never be used to dictate your life, it can be useful to see how your energies might be affected or influenced, which in turn can help you prepare for what life might throw your way.

By the end of these 15 months, these two sections should have given you a deeper understanding and awareness of yourself and, in turn, the world around you. There are never any certainties in life, but with an open mind you will find guidance for what might be, and learn to take more control of your own destiny.

THE CHARACTER OF THE SCALES

. . . .

Symbolised by scales, Libra is a sign of grace and harmony. It is the serene dove carrying an olive branch that offers peace to the zodiac calendar. Librans themselves often act as a cooling breeze that can diffuse even the most heated of situations with diplomacy and charm. Ruled by bright and beautiful Venus, their exquisite good looks leave admirers breathless. Whether they are breaking the internet like Kim Kardashian or stunning the screen like Brigitte Bardot, Librans have characteristically balanced features that are often connected to their fortune. While their personal appearance is important to them, Librans are also skilled at creating beauty too. The scales might therefore tip in their favour if they wish to pursue a creative career in art, architecture, fashion or design.

Born at the start of autumn with a unique cardinal and air combination, Librans are some of the most pioneering thinkers. Whether people agree with them or not, their cardinal attitude has them actively striving for what they believe to be fair. However, rising to the top of their profession can be lonely for Librans, who are not content to have only their shadow for company. Born in the seventh house, which focuses on finding a partner, Librans will need to find the eggs to their bacon, the pen to their paper, the weights to their scales in order to feel the peace and beauty that they are so intent on bringing to others.

SCALES

The scales of justice are an enduring symbol used by courts and legal systems the world over, which makes them the perfect representation for fair-thinking Librans. Whether they're working as lawyers or campaigning as activists, they often feel strongly about their need to rectify any injustices – whether the issues directly affect them or not. The world should get ready for the weight of Librans, as they try their best to strike a balance for everyone. Civil rights activist Mahatma Gandhi is the perfect example of this; originally a barrister, he led a non-violent movement towards the ideals of peace and freedom that inspired, and continues to inspire, millions of people. Librans like to weigh up all their options before making a decision, so don't expect any hasty judgements. Whether it's deciding between two potential partners or between the beef and chicken, Librans can be plagued with indecision, and may evade picking a side to avoid upsetting anyone. Finding equilibrium can be difficult, but these careful and considered types will usually judge fairly. Life is a balancing act for everyone, but especially so for Librans.

VENUS

One of the brightest objects in the sky, beautiful Venus is Libra's ruling planet. Guided by the planet of love and born in the seventh house of relationships, Librans often feel destined to find companionship and settle down. Venus is the hottest planet in the solar system and is named after the Roman goddess of beauty, which may well be why Librans have a reputation for being so attractive. While beauty is in the eye of the beholder, there will typically be something aesthetic about Librans that catches the admiration of potential partners, such as their charming wit or the beauty that they can capture in a poem, painting or floral arrangement. Venus is associated with fertility, which could link to every Libran's love of being outdoors, as well as their positive energy that feeds off external stimulation. Spending quality time soaking up the beauty of nature or stargazing to try and spot their shining planet of Venus may be where Librans find their one true love.

ELEMENTS, MODES AND POLARITIES

Each sign is made up of a unique combination of three defining groups: elements, modes and polarities. Each of these defining parts can manifest themselves in good and bad ways and none should be seen as a positive or a negative – including the polarities! Just like a jigsaw puzzle, piecing these groups together can help illuminate why each sign has certain characteristics and help us find a balance.

ELEMENTS

Fire: Dynamic and adventurous, signs with fire in them are often extroverted. Others are naturally drawn to them because of the positive light they give off, as well as their high levels of energy and confidence.

Earth: Signs with the earth element are steady and driven. They make for solid friends, parents and partners due to their grounded influence and nurturing nature.

Air: The invisible element that influences each of the other elements significantly, air signs provide much-needed perspective to those around them with their fair thinking, verbal skills and key ideas.

Water: Warm in the shallows but sometimes freezing as ice, the emotional depth and empathy of this mysterious element is essential to the growth of everything around it.

MODES

Cardinal: Pioneers of the calendar, cardinal signs jump-start each season and are the energetic go-getters.

Fixed: Marking the middle of the calendar, fixed signs firmly denote and value both steadiness and reliability.

Mutable: As the seasons end, the mutable signs adapt and gladly give themselves over to the promise of change.

POLARITIES

Positive: Typically extroverted, positive signs take physical action and embrace external stimulus in their life.

Negative: Usually introverted, negative signs value emotional development and experiencing life from the inside out.

LIBRA IN BRIEF

The table below shows the key attributes of Librans.
Use it for quick reference and to understand more about this fascinating sign.

SYMBOL	RULING PLANET	MODE	ELEMENT	HOUSE
♎	♀	∧	△	Ⅶ
Scales	Venus	Cardinal	Air	Seventh

COLOURS	BODY PART	POLARITY	GENDER	POLAR SIGN
	🧍	⊕	♂	♈
Pastel Colours	Kidneys	Positive	Masculine	Aries

ROMANTIC RELATIONSHIPS

· · · · · · · · · · · · · · · · ·

Look straight ahead because it's nothing but blue skies for Librans in love. Filled from the inside out with beauty and charm by the influence of their ruling planet Venus, the allure of ever-graceful Librans is felt by many. These artistic types usually have exceptional taste and their style is always impeccable, so whether they're blessed in the looks department or not, there will likely be something visually appealing that catches the attention of others.

Finding that special someone can be essential for Librans to feel whole. To them, being alone may feel as much fun as a seesaw with only one person on it, a situation that couldn't be worse for these seekers of balance. Whether it's through their beauty or their charm, Librans will actively seek out relationships and may discover that love finds them frequently. Belonging to the seventh house in the zodiac calendar, which represents relationships and contracts, wedding bells are likely to chime loudly and clearly for loved-up Librans. In fact, their big day will be planned to perfection, with white doves released on cue.

A partnership is where Librans usually feel most content, with someone by their side to provide constant stimulation. They seek peace and harmony, and are experts at being tactful and finding compromise. Despite all this, their relationships will not be without conflict. When Librans pick a fight, it is a sure sign that they are really unhappy about something. These pacifists are most definitely lovers and not fighters, so try talking problems through openly.

ARIES: COMPATIBILITY 5/5

A polarity is complementary for any star-sign pairing. An Arian and Libran can form a real yin and yang kind of love. The Libran's air element may make the Arian's flames burn that much brighter, while the Libran is best known for bringing harmony and balance into the world, making them an ideal partner for the often-combative Arian. In this partnership of opposites, each can learn from the other in areas that they are lacking. The Libran encouraging the Arian to communicate, while the Arian inspires the Libran to take action.

TAURUS: COMPATIBILITY 4/5

Both ruled by the planet Venus, the love that a Taurean and Libran share can be a thing of beauty. Their joint appreciation of culture and aesthetics will have romance blooming quickly. Wedding bells may ring in both the Taurean and Libran's ears, and planning for the big day could begin sooner rather than later. The Libran's airy indecisiveness may be a point of contention for the grounded Taurean, and these two won't be without their disagreements. However, the Libran's diplomacy will help to resolve issues and have them striving for a harmonious partnership once more.

GEMINI: COMPATIBILITY 3/5

With Libra ruled by the planet of love, Venus, and Gemini by the planet of communication, Mercury, this partnership will be founded on affection and understanding. The debate-loving Geminian and peace-seeking Libran will likely have their conflicts. If love troubles do arise, these two should have the verbal skills and creative thinking to work out their issues. Both can have trouble making up their minds, but the Libran's cardinal instinct usually sets in to help make the course of action clear, much to the delight of the mutable Geminian.

CANCER: COMPATIBILITY 3/5

Ruled by the planet of love and the emotions of the moon, the romance between a Libran and Cancerian can read like an epic poem. The Libran's love for aesthetics will be particularly attractive to the creative Crab and could encourage many shared artistic endeavours. The home that these two build together may well be a thing of beauty and harmony. Both cardinal characters, the Libran and Cancerian match each other's energetic attitudes, but may fight for power in the relationship. While their introvert and extrovert tendencies could clash, the Libran's search for peace may help make this relationship last.

LEO: COMPATIBILITY 4/5

Sitting two places apart on the calendar, a Libran and Leonian can share a compatible partnership. The Libran is an expert in diplomacy, so will likely be able to handle the more dramatic moments in this love affair without bruising the Leonian's ego. Love with the Leonian can be a rollercoaster: fun, but also full of ups and downs. The Libran, symbolised by scales, will hopefully bring a balance to the relationship that the reliable Leonian will appreciate. Ruled by the Sun and Venus, the Leonian and Libran are capable of forming a relationship that is filled with warmth and love.

VIRGO: COMPATIBILITY 3/5

Both advocates of diplomacy and justice, a Libran and Virgoan's love should be fair and true. If these two make vows together, they will take them very seriously. However, it is not all about contracts in this relationship, as the Mercury-inspired Virgoan and Venus-ruled Libran both have a shared love of beauty and crafts. A date night at a gallery or the theatre would be perfect for the art-loving Virgoan and Libran couple. The Libran will have plenty of ideas, while the practical Virgoan could be the one that helps make those fancies a reality.

LIBRA: COMPATIBILITY 5/5

The love between two Librans can be sheer bliss. As a creative coupling, they will be each other's muses and inspire one another to bring beauty into the relationship. This is in no way a shallow meeting of minds, as these two great thinkers share air as their element and are likely to be brimming with ideas and intellect. This luxury-loving pair enjoy delicious dinners and gorgeous gifts, but need to be wary of overindulgence. Overall, the two Librans should easily find the balance and harmony that they both strive for in this partnership of true equals.

SCORPIO: COMPATIBILITY 2/5

When the planets align for Scorpio and Libra, the combination of loving Venus, passionate Mars and powerful Pluto can create an intimate and stimulating love affair. Scorpio's emotions and the mindfulness of the Libran makes for a harmonious pairing, so long as they are both on the same page. The Libran may seem superficial to deep-feeling Scorpio, but thankfully the Libran's charm and diplomacy will help calm any troubled waters if they fail to understand one another. This love won't be without conflicts, but it has the potential to be loyal and long lasting.

SAGITTARIUS: COMPATIBILITY 4/5

With compatible ruling planets of Jupiter and Venus, a Sagittarian and Libran could be very lucky in love together. Their complementary elements of fire and air will no doubt spark a highly passionate union, full of excitement and intimacy. They are both likely to be brimming with positive energy, so should have no problem keeping up with a packed social schedule. The tactful Libran and blunt Sagittarian could clash if their ideas about commitment don't match, but they have a good chance of working out their differences and moving forward happily together. Many adventures await.

CAPRICORN: COMPATIBILITY 1/5

A sure-footed Capricornian and high-spirited Libran have little shared ground and may struggle to strike a balance in love. However, the possibility of a relationship shouldn't be ruled out entirely. Born in the seventh house of relationships, the Libran may struggle if the Capricornian, born in the tenth house of careers, puts work before love, so reaching a compromise here will be essential for a happy union. It will be hard to find equality in this earth/air match, especially when their differences are so plentiful. However, it is possible for this pair to overcome any problems if they are committed enough.

AQUARIUS: COMPATIBILITY 5/5

It can be a whirlwind romance when an Aquarian and Libran fall in love. Ruled by Venus and Uranus, this may well be a rebellious or radical type of relationship. The cardinal Libran is quick to come up with ideas, while the Aquarian's fixed mode makes it possible to bring these ideas to life. Teamwork really does make the dream work for this outgoing, positive couple. The Aquarian's ideals paired with the Libran's sense of righteousness means that this pair have the potential to form a couple that will break down boundaries and create new rules for a utopian future.

PISCES: COMPATIBILITY 2/5

While an enigmatic Piscean and suave Libran might be charmed by one another, theirs is a love that will struggle to reach fruition. The cardinal Libran is more likely to be the initiator in the relationship than the mutable Piscean, but both can be struck with an inability to make decisions, leaving the pair treading water, neither sinking nor swimming. The Libran will be attracted to the artistic side of the creative Piscean, while the Piscean is likely to flourish under the Libran's enthusiastic encouragement. If a balance can be found between the Libran's extrovert tendencies and the Piscean's introvert nature, romance is possible.

FAMILY AND FRIENDS

. . . .

Librans are friends to all. These diplomats are often the peacekeepers in their circle of friends and family, although they are unlikely to take sides, preferring instead to remain neutral. Ultimate peace providers and avoiders of aggression, Librans long to bypass conflict, which can sometimes mean that they sacrifice too much for the sake of a quiet life. While letting bossy Leonian friends choose the film on movie night may not seem like a big deal, Librans should avoid compromising what is truly important to them. They can sometimes be pushovers, but allowing their friends and family to walk all over them will clash with their inherent need for equality. They should therefore try to not be too docile in relationships and be confident when pushing back or saying no.

Being friends with light-hearted Librans can be a complete joy. They are sure to have an uplifting effect on their friends and family, whether it's chatting with Virgoans over a cup of coffee or persuading their homebody Cancerian friends to come out partying with them late into the night. Librans can at times be a little flaky and may fail to do what they said they would. However, they often make up for their unreliability by showering friends and family with beautiful gifts. If Librans ever find themselves short of money, they will instead be generous with their time and love – the value of which their family and friends are sure to be grateful for.

Whether it's visiting art galleries, starting a book club or getting the best seats in the house for that stunning new show, arty Librans are the refined comrades that keep their friends up to date with all the latest art and cultural affairs. A visit to a Libran house might feel like stepping straight into a gallery, as it is bound to be filled with beautiful objects and design. Taureans, also ruled by Venus, will be more than happy to stop round for a glass of fine wine or two, while the attention to beautiful detail will also not go unnoticed by Virgoans.

When it comes to family, Librans can thrive in any environment that involves a partnership, so parenting may come naturally to them. While they will enjoy spoiling their children, they will also be keen to instil the importance of sharing and playing fairly with others. Libran offspring may have the latest toys, but they'll need to play nicely if they want to hold on to them. Generous Librans always prefer to be sympathetic to their children and may shy away from disciplining any bad behaviour. Learning how to take on the role of both good cop and bad cop will be beneficial in creating a balanced family unit.

MONEY AND CAREERS

. . . .

Being a particular star sign will not dictate certain types of career, but it can help to identify potential areas to thrive in. To succeed in the workplace, it is important to understand your strengths and weaknesses, which will help in choosing and achieving career and financial goals.

While balance is key for Librans, managing money might be a bit of a struggle for them. Tempted to choose the most beautiful things in life, such as tickets to the opera or a new designer outfit, a Libran's budget may fly out of the window in the pursuit of beauty. Despite being great thinkers, these lovers of luxury usually don't have a flair for funds. Making an effort to sit down and work out their financial affairs, or perhaps even finding someone else to do it, could be essential for keeping Librans out of their overdrafts, and won't prevent them from being able to enjoy the occasional treat.

With an innate sense of both beauty and justice, careers in design or law are two fields that Librans may flourish in. They are known for their great taste and glamour, so a career in which aesthetics are important, such as fashion, theatre or beauty, could be where they are naturally drawn. Walking down the catwalk, like famous Libran model Bella Hadid, or designing clothes, like Donna Karan, may be dream jobs. Alternatively, language or music may be just as appealing for Librans, especially if they are disinclined towards public image. Oscar Wilde and T.S. Eliot ably demonstrate how words can create a picture as rich and beautiful as graphic art, while Franz Liszt and Ray Charles are fine examples of the spectrum of musical talent Librans could possess if so inclined. If the courthouse is more appealing than the catwalk, working in the justice system could be the perfect fit for diplomatic Librans. Working as judges, activists or lawyers, Librans can contribute to restoring the balance of justice in the world. Whether it's using their profile to make the world a better place, like Bob Geldof, or ensuring fairness and justice are delivered directly, like Judge Judy, Librans strive for a greater good. Librans are often comfortable in the public eye, be it in politics or show business, and can count presidents and Oscar winners amongst their ranks. They love to entertain, and making people happy fits neatly with their drive to make the world a better place for everyone.

Reasonable and cooperative, Librans make for the fairest of bosses, and will work hard to create a tranquil environment for their employees to thrive in. If their colleagues are feeling disgruntled, Librans will find solutions to fix the problem. They are unlikely to tolerate gossip or unfair behaviour in the workplace, and will quickly extinguish it if they catch wind of it. Whether it's managing an office of people or refereeing a sports game, the rulings of Librans are fair and final.

As with family, colleagues cannot be chosen. Therefore, it can be advantageous to use star signs to learn about their key characteristics and discover the best ways of working together. Partnerships are integral to Librans, so finding kindred work colleagues can really help them take flight in their careers. Sharing the element of air, Geminians and Aquarians will connect with Librans on a thoughtful level, and can make inspiring and influential colleagues. Libran John Lennon and Geminian Paul McCartney are a great example of the dizzying heights of success that these two deep thinkers can help each other reach together.

HEALTH AND WELLBEING

. . . .

Finding serenity is essential for peaceful Librans, so stressful situations can be particularly damaging to them. At times, these high-flyers might start to feel detached from both the people around them and their day-to-day routines, particularly if they live in a built-up area. A change of scenery may help Librans shed some of that restlessness; a walk to the top of a hill or to the beach, or anywhere their element of air can freely whip around them, should help restore calmness. Meditation is another technique that Librans could try to ease their worries. Breathing exercises are a particularly effective calming method, and are quick and easy enough to practise while on the move. By taking at least three deep breaths in a row, they should feel the panic lift and rational thoughts return once more.

Librans are usually great thinkers, but while some will find answers quickly, others may get stuck in a painful mental state of constant indecision. The chance to bounce ideas off colleagues or a partner is one reason why Librans always like to have company, especially if it makes finalising plans easier for them. Such is their hatred of being the lone decision-maker, Librans may instead end up flipping a coin. However, they should remind themselves that they possess the rationale required to make sound judgements. While they may argue that two heads are always better than one, being confident to make up their own minds may have the double benefit of helping them feel more comfortable with their own company. Librans may do well to realise that they don't necessarily need a partner for everything.

Music can be a powerful healer for Librans, whether they are the musician, like fellow Librans John Lennon and Bruce Springsteen, or they are the listener. Simply enjoying their favourite artists or an inspiring playlist after a hard day could help lift their mood. They may want to take their love of music one step further by hitting the dance floor and letting off some steam. If Librans can't convince their friends to grab their dancing shoes and meet them at the club, then joining a dance class at a gym or studio could be a great way of regularly experiencing the joys of music and dance. Engaging in physical activities that combine both their love of socialising and music is likely to be a winning combination for Librans.

Libra

....

DAILY FORECASTS
for 2022

OCTOBER

Saturday 1st

Challenges might cause you to down tools and go on strike today. It wouldn't hurt to distance yourself from others now. Immerse yourself in your own hobbies and interests; there'll be time to reconnect and help others when you've fulfilled your own needs.

Sunday 2nd

If family issues persist, you may have to step into a position of authority today. Mercury turns direct, so you'll need to tie up some loose ends. Try not to let your responsibilities overwhelm you. Get enough rest.

Monday 3rd

You may need to be the one in your family who suggests that the past be laid to rest. Don't forget to mention that the future is something to look forward to. This afternoon is good for stirring things up in the best possible way. Some emotional pruning might be necessary.

Tuesday 4th

Working with others will help you to be productive today. Mental challenges are easier to overcome when part of a team. You're likely to have a good ear for what's fair, so listen to all involved and find a harmonious way to co-create or do some good in the world. Be open to the innovative and the unusual.

Wednesday 5th

Restless energy can be a catalyst for change if you use it wisely. Don't be tempted to go off and do your own thing. Stick to the rules and be respectful of the wisdom of those who have more experience. Think everything through and you may hit your targets today.

Thursday 6th

Shift your focus today. You may feel more sensitive and compassionate about your close groups. Ask how you can be of service to others without compromising yourself. It's a good idea to stay open and flexible. Do something good for your body, such as exercise or eating a healthy meal.

Friday 7th

Listen carefully to your inner voice today. It's possible that you get a better idea of what your mission or personal quest should be, and this might mean that you need to cut ties with something involving the family. Reinventing the rule book might be the way forward.

Saturday 8th

If you have a gut feeling that you're on the right track today, listen to it and ignore the little voice inside that is critical or doubtful. If you feel emotionally overloaded this evening, spend time being good to yourself. Try to have some fun with a partner by doing something you both enjoy.

Sunday 9th

Pluto turns direct today and could give you some respite from any building or rebuilding you've been doing within your family. A full moon in your relationship zone also highlights everything you've achieved in the last six months. Stop, slow down and think about discarding anything that has weighed your relationship down.

Monday 10th

A detox or declutter of your inner mind would be good now. File away the negative stuff or discard it completely. A fresh viewpoint will help you to move on and grow. Consider being direct about what you want from your relationship.

Tuesday 11th

Don't be surprised if you are called upon to be a spokesperson, mediator or teacher today. Any logical decision making will be easier if you can cut through the nonsense and see the truth.

Wednesday 12th

You're unlikely to have the energy to pursue extracurricular activities today. Stick to one thing and see it through to the end, as it could become a burden if you procrastinate. If you get irritable, do something relaxing such as meditation or yoga. Still your mind, and your heart will follow.

Thursday 13th

Try to connect with people who inspire you. You may need a nudge or a call to venture beyond your limits today. Communicating with people you've lost touch with can be good for your soul and will entice you to research, study or engage with cultures that are unfamiliar to you.

Friday 14th

Creativity and romance get a boost today. You may be working with something new and finding out what you can and can't do. This should feel more like a fun challenge and will replenish your energy. If this is about romance, try to have a playful time getting to know someone.

Saturday 15th

Your drive and passion may combine to make a day of high productivity. This should soothe your soul and be just what you need to feel safe, nurtured and homely. Treat yourself to a tasty meal this evening or watch some of your favourite movies with people you care about.

Sunday 16th

Pay attention to your thoughts today and make note of any triggers that occur. There may be some childhood conditioning that needs to be dealt with. For example, something that once served as a survival mechanism may no longer be good enough. Don't take on anything new today as you will likely get bored with it immediately.

Monday 17th

You may feel exposed and under attack today. This is probably an old habitual response, so try not to take things personally. You could be feeling vulnerable, but you may also be experiencing passive aggression and react to it negatively. Take a step back and refrain from engaging.

Tuesday 18th

Your courage returns today, so you can be more outgoing now. However, you may also be childlike and stubbornly refuse to conform. How you behave today could impact your significant relationship, so be careful. Fiery energy can lead to tears and tantrums. Get support from your close friends and groups.

Wednesday 19th

A poor mood could continue into this evening, preventing you from getting anything done. You might clash with authority figures or completely discard a creative project you've put a lot of time into. Underneath the surface, you might discover that your desire and drive are working together.

Thursday 20th

You should try to find more of a balance and be able to draw on your natural talents to come out on top today. Perhaps you're showcasing what you're made and are recognised as a leader in your groups. People will look up to you today, so don't let them down.

Friday 21st

Quality time by yourself will be good for you today. Reflect on what you have made room for over the course of the year. Cleaning up your environment, your mind and your body can be a positive step towards manifesting more of your goals and intentions. Get introspective and spiritual.

Saturday 22nd

You may wish to tweak the balance or redirect your inner compass today. Leave a gap in your schedule to think about what you want to achieve next. Don't overwhelm yourself, but be choosy. Try not to feel burdened with obligations to others.

Sunday 23rd

Today could be a game changer. Your ruler, Venus, is in the heart of the Sun and is powering up to be her best self. For you, this means that self-love, pleasure, harmony and money will become a priority. Saturn turns direct and relieves you of restrictions in romance and creativity.

Monday 24th

Your head and heart are likely to be in agreement today. You may usually have a good sense of when things are discordant, but today everything should feel in sync. Enjoy this moment of calm and consider where your next move will take you. Maintain the equilibrium for now.

Tuesday 25th

A seductive time is ahead of you, so reach out and embrace it. A new moon and a solar eclipse will entice you to go after what you want. Your heart's desires may seem indulgent, but remember that an eclipse causes strange energy, so nothing is certain or set.

Wednesday 26th

You may experience unusually intense feelings today, especially if the past comes back into your awareness. You may feel grief or regret stirring your emotions. This is a dark road which you would be advised to stay away from. Close your eyes and leave it all behind you.

Thursday 27th

Your mind may be full of ideas and plans now, but they need to make their way onto your vision board or into a filing cabinet before you can do anything about them. Seeing them in a corner of your mind every day might undo all the cleaning you've done. Aim to be direct in your communication.

Friday 28th

Be incredibly careful today, as something could come along that adds to your daily duties and threatens to weigh you down again. You may feel as if something has been removed from your relationship zone and added elsewhere. Keep your boundaries strong and healthy and say no to extra duties.

Saturday 29th

Conversations might become muddled or misunderstood today, so take your time when explaining or comprehending something. You may have the energy to go the extra mile in your studies, but make sure you don't miss out on important information. Take this day hour by hour and listen carefully to instructions. Check that your finances are in order.

Sunday 30th

You might feel especially attached to your possessions now and be thinking about splashing the cash on a luxury item. Mars turns retrograde today, forcing you to review your commitment to study, travel and personal connections. Slow down and look at the bigger picture over the next few months.

Monday 31st

A necessary change may occur in your home and family zone today, but it won't be a big issue, even if you're the instigator. A collective effort might be required to uncover something important, and this might be uncomfortable.

NOVEMBER

. . . .

Tuesday 1st

If today is challenging, the trick is not to let it get to you, even if your creative and romantic pursuits feel stifled. Don't give up, and instead take a rest stop to evaluate what you've achieved so far. If you find that you're frustrated, do physical exercise or other grounding activities.

Wednesday 2nd

Slow down your thinking today. If you persist in trying to solve a problem, you may get confused and make mistakes. Do what's necessary, then leave the rest until you have more clarity. This evening you might prefer to switch off and do something relaxing. You may find that you reminisce.

Thursday 3rd

Your emotions might be on the surface today, but this could also mean that you're able to go with the flow. Get to the bottom of a problem and put your mind to issues that involve your money, self-worth and what you have around you. Dream something beautiful into being.

Friday 4th

Hold your inner compass tightly today and survey the scenery. You could be realigning with your core values or discover that spiritual matters interest you now. You may wonder about the big life questions and ask yourself where you fit in. What is your role? What else is out there for you?

Saturday 5th

Partner time is favoured over the weekend. You might notice a shift, and this could be partly due to what you've let go of. Losing excess baggage can give you a better perspective on what remains. There may still be something you need to discard, and this will be tough.

Sunday 6th

Romance may occur on a more mature level today, and you might also be able to relate to someone in ways that are more helpful and respectful. Fuel your passions and keep a low fire burning between you both. A small issue within your family could lead you to investigate past discussions for any falsities or incongruities.

Monday 7th

Your energy is likely to turn inward today. Concentrate on making something concrete and look at how the seeds of your dreams are doing now. Go deeper into your psyche and be more discerning about what fascinates you. Remember your self-worth and don't let those in authority try to dumb you down or offer unsatisfactory compromises.

Tuesday 8th

A full moon and a lunar eclipse close a window on a strange period. However, you may still be down a rabbit hole and need directions to get out. Your best guide is your inner voice, so be rational and logical today. Be aware that your emotions could play tricks on you.

. . . .

Wednesday 9th

Another internal shift might cause you a lot of discomfort today. You may experience jealousy, tempers and a blow to your ego. Intense feelings can knock your confidence. Give this a lot of thought before reacting. Ask for advice or confide in a close friend who will support you.

Thursday 10th

Be mindful of your conversations today. There may be harsh words or gossip going around. This may not necessarily be about you, but something you witness. For example, someone could be trying to discredit another person. Draw on self-love and personal ethics to get through this.

Friday 11th

Racing to meet deadlines could get you into trouble today. As keen as you may be to complete a project, rushing can cause you to miss things. An emotional attachment to something might make you feel angry or frustrated. Stick to the rules and pace yourself. Breathe deeply if you feel anxious.

Saturday 12th

A weekend spent under the duvet with your favourite books, food and movies could be just what you need. You must balance your mood, and the best way to do so is to nurture your inner child. Have fun doing childlike things or get cosy with your family. Work can wait.

Sunday 13th

Your mood should lighten as you rejoin the grown-up world. It's fun to play, but you're likely to have chores that you can't ignore today. Empathy, compassion and deeply felt connections are on the agenda.

Monday 14th

Look at your security needs today. Your finances could be a big part of this, so keep a close eye on your savings. You might find that you're offered a bonus and already know how you want to spend it. Be brave and express yourself now.

Tuesday 15th

If something has caught your eye, such as a new opportunity or an item for your home, you may be going all out to get it. Remember that it's possible to treat yourself without tipping into excess. Think twice before you make an impulse buy you might regret later.

Wednesday 16th

Venus moves signs today and will make you more determined to travel, communicate and seek a higher truth. You may be connecting with people who can help to advance you in your career goals. Make one small dream a reality today.

Thursday 17th

Research and mundane chores will keep you occupied today. You may be scheming away in the background, aiming your sights far and wide. Clean up a messy spot and check in with your body's needs. Alone time will clear your mind and help you work through your chores.

Friday 18th

It's possible that you feel irritable or restless today. You may visualise your inner compass but find that it's out of reach. Maybe something has been knocked off balance and needs realigning. Get busy with practical activities to take your mind off other projects, which might be going slower than you'd like.

Saturday 19th

The moon drops into your sign today, and its energy should put you back on an even keel. Connecting with siblings or interacting with your local community is often satisfying and can even open your eyes to a good cause. A short day trip may be enjoyable now.

Sunday 20th

A nice balance of home, work and play can help you to march through the day with confidence. Knowing that you have nothing to tick off your to-do list is always a good feeling. You may be able to return to your romantic and creative endeavours with a more mature attitude now.

Monday 21st

If there are deadlines to meet today, this could leave you feeling flustered. Slowly does it, as you may miss something important if you rush. You might be finalising an issue within your family or taking an objective look at what needs to be done next. Tricky conversations need to be handled with compassion to get the desired results.

Tuesday 22nd

Finances or issues around your self-worth have the potential to be healed today. You may receive an unpleasant reminder of a past experience. This might be an old problem regarding jealousy that still has the power to make you react in a childlike manner, even after all this time.

Wednesday 23rd

Look at how you interact with others today. This could be about joining in with group work or doing the mundane chores you do to get through the day. Your sense of responsibility will tell you that these things are important to maintain good relationships. Don't dismiss your value.

Thursday 24th

A new moon allows you to think about how you can explore the wider world. With Jupiter turning direct today, the world awaits you. This is a great day for booking vacations, starting a course of education or adding to your skills. For example, you could consider learning a new language.

Friday 25th

You might feel as if you're in a haze today, and your mood could be hard to pin down. Do what's necessary and aim to be flexible. If something isn't working, come back to it with fresh eyes another day. Family and tradition may need your attention over the weekend.

Saturday 26th

Today is good for connecting with those closest to you. There may be a family meeting that reveals important matters or secrets. Try to deal with this responsibly and respectfully. You may even be the one who acts as a mediator or is called upon to negotiate when others have trouble.

Sunday 27th

Be there for others today. If you can bring a new perspective to the table, this will be appreciated. A big change could be happening, so someone may need to guide and nurture the more anxious members of your family. Take on this role, and others will feel supported by you.

Monday 28th

You can be open-minded and ambitious today. Working slowly and methodically will give you positive energy to deal with anything that comes your way. It's a good idea to use your mental skills to discern and explore options where possible. If you bring work home with you, be aware of the possibility that you might fail to be productive in your own environment.

Tuesday 29th

If you're waiting for a breakthrough, you may not get it today. Find other ways of dealing with a problem. Networking with those who have experience can help you learn something to your advantage. Distractions such as phone calls or mundane conversations may impede your progress this evening.

Wednesday 30th

Reach out to people who can be useful to you. This might be in a romantic, educational or creative way. You may find that you need to call in a few favours. Notice the flow of give and take and recognise how beneficial it can be.

DECEMBER

. . . .

Thursday 1st

You may have a tricky start to the day, so you will need to be adaptable. Your inner compass is there to remind you that forging ahead with something without thinking can sometimes cause mistakes. Be patient with anyone who is not as quick to understand something as you are.

Friday 2nd

Be mindful of your partner's needs today. You may be racing ahead just as they need you to slow down. However, this could be a good thing if you're organising an activity that they have been procrastinating about. They might need a gentle nudge to make a decision.

Saturday 3rd

You're likely to have fiery energy today, and this could make you impatient. You may need to check in with people you've neglected recently, and you should have enough energy to deal with any blockages or restrictions. Take the lead and achieve something small, or find a creative solution to a problem.

Sunday 4th

Neptune turns direct today, so you should notice that you have more clarity and can plan your mundane duties more effectively. You might not be ready to factor in your dreams and visions just yet, but you can review them and see if they still suit you. Make time for pleasure this afternoon.

Monday 5th

You may sense that something has been left unsaid today, perhaps regarding a grand gesture or an act of kindness. You might also have an epiphany that provides more direction on your personal path. Restless energy might rake up an issue from your private life.

Tuesday 6th

A sleepless night could be the result of your mind doing overtime. Problems often appear bigger than they are, so take some time to put things into perspective. If you look at all the options, you might find the solution. Taking small steps can help you tackle a big task.

Wednesday 7th

You might sense the planetary energy urging you to make decisions now. These may concern travel, higher education or networking with long-distance contacts. Don't let the pressure get to you: all will be made easier soon. You can conquer a huge task if you break it down into smaller pieces.

Thursday 8th

The full moon will boost the energy you have available to manage extracurricular activities, especially if you have received confirmation of an opportunity you've been waiting for. Now you need to slim things down to make them fit in with your lifestyle and other obligations. If things don't feel right, perhaps you shouldn't go ahead.

Friday 9th

You won't get much done if you're hiding in your comfort zone, but it might be necessary to do so if you need to protect yourself. You may be feeling vulnerable, especially if you have some doubts about your abilities. Try not to listen to your inner critic, and instead aim to soothe your inner child and nurture yourself. You may just need familial support.

Saturday 10th

Venus enters your family zone, and this means that you should be able to deal with any issues more compassionately. While you might sometimes feel the need to be strict, you can ease off now. Ensure that those around you thrive.

Sunday 11th

This could be a gentle and sensitive day for you. Your intuition is likely to be high, so listen to what it has to say. You might have to put your own needs last, but this could be a positive thing if it connects you with your core values.

Monday 12th

You may find yourself adding your voice to a group effort or a good cause today. Laughing and being playful can bring a good vibe to your day, and all around you will benefit. Doing so can also add a spark to your romance and artistic projects.

Tuesday 13th

Be careful that your positive mood doesn't turn into selfishness today. You might find that someone doesn't agree with your candid behaviour, and this could cause a clash. Put that energy into reaching out and catching up with long-lost friends. You might like to organise a festive event for your group.

Wednesday 14th

As your mood turns inward, you might notice that you are more methodical and can process your thoughts more easily. Alone time will be beneficial now. You may be writing lists and getting prepared for the upcoming celebrations, and a healthy mindset will help over this busy period.

Thursday 15th

Practical activities can boost your wellbeing. Knuckle down and work through your tasks consistently. Being productive and organised is good for your home and your soul. Make contact with others and ensure that they are aware of what's expected of them. If you need to shake things up, do so.

Friday 16th

Go easy on yourself today and remember that not everyone is as organised as you. If others fail to toe the line, you may feel exasperated and try to make changes by yourself. If this helps you to feel satisfied, then it isn't necessarily a bad thing.

Saturday 17th

You may feel resentful if family members aren't pulling their weight today, and it might be difficult to be as pleasant as usual to some. Try to let this go and make sure that your own needs are met instead. An event with your group of friends may be just what you need to let off steam.

Sunday 18th

You may be inclined to pay attention to your romantic and creative activities today. Just make sure that all your chores are done first, as this will free up time to enjoy your hobbies later. If you need to redress the balance of work and play, get creative and have some fun.

Monday 19th

Use your role in the family to consider what needs to be adjusted or discarded today. There may be a situation or a past event you've enjoyed together which can be revived. Perhaps your family once enjoyed a festive tradition that can now be introduced to younger members.

Tuesday 20th

Jupiter returns to your relationship zone, where it will stay for some time. Opportunities will grow for you now as a result of this cosmic shift, and you may travel together with a partner more this coming year. Allow yourselves to dream big and don't hesitate to try something new. This could be the year to take your relationship to the next level.

Wednesday 21st

The winter solstice arrives, and the shortest day of sunlight is a time to reflect. Gather your thoughts, resources and friends for the long nights ahead. Think about what brings quality to your life and do more of that.

Thursday 22nd

You might feel the year winding down and want to lock yourself away with a partner or an artistic project you wish to finish. If you notice a shift in your energy, bend yourself towards it and go with the flow.

Friday 23rd

A new moon in your family zone makes this the perfect time to reaffirm your commitments to yourself. Traditional family values are important at this time of year and should be passed on to the younger generations, as doing so can be greatly rewarding and beneficial.

Saturday 24th

The planetary energy is perfect for connecting and having a harmonious time with those closest to you. There may be some anticipation or restlessness, but this is to be expected. Notice and enjoy how aligned you feel right now. Remember this feeling in the future when you need to rebalance yourself.

Sunday 25th

You may be more in tune with today's energy than you think. Enjoy a day of generosity, romance and real connection with your loved ones and the world in general. If you feel extremely optimistic for the year ahead, pass this feeling onto others. Group efforts will make the day go well.

Monday 26th

It's possible that you overdid things and now need time to get back on form. If you need to be alone, no one will blame you. You might feel more like getting back into the swing of the season by the evening, but it's also important to stay within your personal limits.

Tuesday 27th

It may be business as usual where your mundane chores are concerned. However, you might also be reflecting on what everything means and seeking a more personal or spiritual connection to the universe. Why not allow yourself to move away from your comfort zone and try something new?

Wednesday 28th

You may spend the day doing something unusual. For example, an invitation could arrive that intrigues you. This may mean trying something you wouldn't normally be comfortable with. Check in with your inner compass and see if this is for you. If this is just what you need, you can think outside the box and challenge yourself.

Thursday 29th

Mercury turns retrograde today, and this could affect matters regarding your family and status. You will need to be crystal clear in your communications to make sure everyone knows what's expected of them. Emotions might be huge today, especially if you're making new rules or agreeing to be more available to your family.

Friday 30th

This can be a tricky day, especially if things feel anticlimactic. If the adrenaline that keeps your motor running is depleted, give yourself time to refuel. Don't do anything excessive or try to make progress where none can be made. Switch off and enjoy some partner time.

Saturday 31st

It's unlikely that anything important will happen today, so you might be better off having downtime and refraining from making commitments. You may wish to celebrate privately and enjoy some luxury or pleasures this evening. Don't get dragged out to a party with family if you're not up to it. Enjoy the close of 2022.

Libra

....

DAILY FORECASTS
for 2023

JANUARY

. . . .

Sunday 1st

It could be an intense start to the new year, perhaps because some of your plans haven't worked out, or because you're experiencing a sense of loss or grief as the year begins. Put your needs first and take a step back from a situation that's causing you pain.

Monday 2nd

You may want to mend some bridges today, perhaps with someone in your family. However, communication planet Mercury remains retrograde in your home and family zone, and this means that misunderstandings are likely. Visualise good relations, but wait before speaking out.

Tuesday 3rd

As a Libra, you're a people person at heart. Once your ruling planet Venus enters Aquarius today, you're going to be in the mood for fun and games. Leave any stresses behind as you play and have fun. Bring out your inner weird and do something outside your comfort zone.

Wednesday 4th

Be actively romantic, chase after love, be flirtatious, prioritise good times and laughter and do more of what you enjoy. This could be one of the standout days of the year for love and romance. Get your teeth into a project that inspires you and shows off your talents.

Thursday 5th

A change of fortune could be the trigger to move on or say goodbye. Someone close could come up with a solution to a home or family issue that's been dragging on. Shine a light on your past and put bad times behind you.

Friday 6th

The lunar light is brightest during the full moon, so this is an ideal time to trust your intuition. Talk things through with your family this weekend and have those big conversations. Don't avoid the issues that need to be addressed, especially around work and home.

Saturday 7th

You may be caring for someone elderly or grieving a loss as the year begins. Emotions will run deep during this full moon period. Aim to let go of resentments and don't get pulled back into the past. Some tough decisions might need to be made.

Sunday 8th

Make sure you have a way to escape from more serious issues. Romance could be on the cards today and socialising will invariably lift your spirits. If someone is pushing you to make a big decision, it might be best to wait until January 18th before doing so.

Monday 9th

Line up some fun adventures with the one you love or your group of best friends. If you're a typical Libra, you love socialising and having fun. Actively engage with life and be around the people who lift your spirits. A holiday could be on the way soon.

Tuesday 10th

Don't be too disheartened if things don't work out today or someone lets you down. Having some time to yourself might turn out to be a good thing, whether you're catching up with admin or choosing to rest.

Wednesday 11th

When it comes to home and family affairs, be aware that nothing is settled or final right now. You can still change your mind, so give yourself one more week to think things through. Someone from your past could reach out and reconnect today.

Thursday 12th

It might be time to find a new sense of meaning or explore your philosophy on life further. If you've felt trapped or claustrophobic recently, reach out to the wider world and do something bold and courageous. Focus on travel and study and think about your future goals.

Friday 13th

The moon is in your star sign, so there's no reason to be superstitious on Friday 13th. Tap into your intuition and trust your inner knowingness. Be wise. Someone's kind gesture this afternoon could restore your faith in humanity.

Saturday 14th

Even though socialising could bring some benefits your way today, you may want something more substantial from life right now. Your planet Venus is in the heat of the action this weekend, so there's a restless feel to your stars which might cause you to crave excitement more than usual.

Sunday 15th

This is a day where anything goes in your close relationships, so you may not find it easy to keep the peace. Be aware that today may bring the unexpected, especially when it comes to love. It's not the best day to try and sort out an issue with someone significant.

Monday 16th

You may be used to money being more of a roller-coaster ride than a steady financial stream in your life. If your indulgent streak kicks in, you might find that you want to spend not save. Keep an eye on your budget.

Tuesday 17th

If something's costing you a lot of money, such as an expensive hobby, you should try to be more aware of this than usual. Consider whether the expense is worth it and talk things through with someone close.

Wednesday 18th

Your home and family zone is under the cosmic spotlight, and it's here where there's the potential for a green light. If you've been waiting for something over the last few weeks, things may take a turn for the better. Crack on with a home or family project with confidence.

Thursday 19th

Mercury, the planet of communication, is now directly in your home and family zone, and this means that you may be able to break free from a situation where you've had little or no control. Alternatively, this could flag up what you need to confront or deal with head-on. Take back your power.

Friday 20th

The Sun enters Aquarius today, and this is good news for you as it means there's less pressure in your home and family zone. A potentially lighter energy may kick in, so you can start to move away from a situation that's held you back. You should experience a strong sense of relief.

Saturday 21st

This is a wonderful weekend to be proactive and initiate events that are packed full of promise and fun. If you're looking for love, it's a great time to reach out to other people. A new moon in Aquarius favours modern technology, so look online and consider joining a dating site if you're single.

Sunday 22nd

Today's stars signify a pivotal moment and will help you to feel ready to make a major decision that influences not only you but also the ones you love. Now is the moment to make a big change for the better in a relationship or friendship.

Monday 23rd

A romance or love affair may develop a serious edge now. Be honest with yourself and others, and don't dismiss your true feelings. Set new rules or boundaries and consider where in life you're being called upon to be more responsible.

Tuesday 24th

Keep the wheels turning and aim to make progress with projects both at work and at home. It's a good idea to keep the lines of communication open and aim to get everyone involved. Prioritise teamwork and ask for support wherever you need it most.

Wednesday 25th

If you're a typical Libra, you often put other people before yourself. Be wary of this tendency today: if you kick into helping mode, you might sacrifice your needs to be of service to others. Having said that, you may gain great benefit from a volunteering or caring role.

Thursday 26th

Other people could be a boon in your life today, so be ready to listen and learn. Notice the people who can help you and lift your spirits. An entrepreneurial, trailblazing individual could open the door to your future success.

Friday 27th

Your ruling planet Venus is on the move today, and enters your work and health zone. This is great for improving relations with work colleagues and using your imagination to boost your job, routine or lifestyle. Don't be afraid to try new things.

Saturday 28th

Your current stars are encouraging you to look after your health and focus on your lifestyle. Decide where you want to invest your energy and do so wisely to boost your wellbeing. The more you put in, the more you get back in return.

Sunday 29th

It's a good day to explore new topics and ideas, such as psychology and astrology. Be open to broadening your perspective on what's possible, as this can only enrich your mind. Trying something new will shift your cosmic energy.

Monday 30th

If you've been trying to make a big decision since the end of last year, give it one more go today. If you know what might help someone close, see if they're willing to take advice, as they may now be less fearful of change.

Tuesday 31st

Your adventurous side may come to the fore today, so embrace a new experience and don't hold back. Whether you're keen to travel somewhere unusual or boost your intelligence, it's an ideal time to challenge yourself. Say yes to life by being bold and courageous.

FEBRUARY

·················

Wednesday 1st

It would be easy to dip into impossibility today. If you find you're dreaming about what you want to do in life but not taking action, try to be constructive by taking one small step towards a long-term goal. It's an ideal day for planning and considering the bigger picture.

Thursday 2nd

The more emotionally involved you are with your job or career, the more fulfilled you'll feel. You may feel yourself being drawn towards a creative or artistic vocation that matters to you deeply. Do what you believe in.

Friday 3rd

If you're not able to pursue your chosen goals because life is too busy, aim to readdress the balance today. This might mean a difficult conversation with a loved one about a tough choice or decision. Notice who or what is holding you back from living your best life.

Saturday 4th

The key area where you're wise to be cautious right now is your finances. Keep close tabs on your money and don't take an impulsive or unnecessary risk. Make sure your possessions are safe and secure.

Sunday 5th

Full moons can make you feel dramatic and emotional, so
you may find that you wear your heart on your sleeve today.
You might fall for someone you know or begin to feel closer
to your best friends. Make time for a party or celebration and
prioritise your social life.

Monday 6th

Ensure you balance your time well this week, especially if
you're busy. Take some time out to destress and relax fully. If
you've been burning the candle at both ends recently, even
more reason to take good care of yourself. Turn to a family
member if you require help or advice.

Tuesday 7th

You could easily feel frustrated if things aren't working out the
way you want them to. Take a step back instead of pushing too
hard, and don't try to do everything by yourself. Ensure you
have a good team around you both at home and at work.

Wednesday 8th

If you're looking for work, this is a good time to line up an
interview or send an application. Use your negotiating skills
to good effect. There might be good news for someone in
the family today that is job-related. Create a strong support
network around you.

. . . .

Thursday 9th

You should feel more settled and less stressed out from today onwards. With the moon in your star sign, you're wise to do whatever's necessary to create more balance and harmony in your life. Look after yourself and try not to give too much of your energy away.

Friday 10th

Today is a good day to have a final conversation with your family that puts an ongoing issue to bed. Once you've all had your say, resolve to close the door on the past so that you can start to move forward.

Saturday 11th

Social planet Mercury enters air sign Aquarius today, so you should feel in your element. Use this astrology to help improve the understanding between yourself and someone close; ring the changes and do something new together.

Sunday 12th

Keep your money safe and secure today and don't get carried away on a whim. If you're often careless or reckless with your finances, even more reason to look after what you have. Appreciate your assets and possessions and learn to value yourself and your skills highly.

Monday 13th

Look at where you can cut costs, especially if you're spending more money than you're earning. Don't lose sight of your ability to learn more about your resources, as doing so can help to ensure you're safe and secure financially.

Tuesday 14th

It's a good week to focus on your routine and on bringing a sense of flow into your life. Actively engage with your work, whether you're chasing a new job or enhancing your team. You can play a pivotal role in bringing people together today.

Wednesday 15th

Look after yourself and put your needs first. If you've been spending a lot of time and energy caring for others, consider readjusting the balance. Alternatively, if you feel it would benefit you to offer your kindness and caring, do so. Sometimes you need to heal yourself before you can help others.

Thursday 16th

You should have discipline and commitment in spades today, even if things feel relentless. You might be continuing with a hobby or craft and want to pursue it more passionately. Think about which creative projects you want to pursue and which you want to abandon.

Friday 17th

Someone close could step in to help you by reminding you of your strengths today. Try to spend some quality time reconnecting with your family. Do what feels right for you. Concentrate on the basics of life rather than getting carried away with overly optimistic plans.

. . . .

Saturday 18th

Go with the flow and see where life leads you today. Be optimistic, focus on fun and play, and bring your artistic and creative nature to your work and routine. Allow your compassionate nature to shine by helping those closest to you.

Sunday 19th

If life has become all work and no play, consider shifting the balance. Relationships might feel more significant in your life from this week onwards. You'll feel unhappy if life is too one-sided, so consider what you need more of and where you can create more space.

Monday 20th

Today's new moon means that it's a good time to set your intentions and decide where you're heading. Notice what's inspiring you and how it brings you happiness and fulfilment. Do more of what you love.

Tuesday 21st

There could be some delights in store if you remain open, receptive and willing to explore today. Practise gratitude daily and notice how doing so improves your general wellbeing. Appreciate the ways that the people in your life can help you achieve your goals.

Wednesday 22nd

Don't hold back if you there is someone that you want to connect with. Reach out to an exciting and adventurous person and let their feel-good spirit rub off on you. It's a good day to get to know someone better.

Thursday 23rd

If you want some new people in your life, now's the time to get out there and meet them. Consider joining a sports group or playing a more active role at your child's school. The more involved you are within your local community, the more connected you will feel to the people around you.

Friday 24th

It's a good idea to double-check your facts and figures today. If you're not sure whether you're being paid the correct amount for a job or your wage slip doesn't add up, pay close attention. Money often equals security, emotionally as well as financially.

Saturday 25th

Check whether your urge to splurge is about a savvy investment or a potential money pit. Even if you're feeling flush, it's not a great day to spend your all money in one place. An impulsive purchase could drain your funds, so do your research before leaping in.

Sunday 26th

Don't avoid having a conversation that could save you money. If something is draining your resources, this could be the time to make a change. A good book or a thought-provoking film could be a welcome escape this evening.

Monday 27th

It's an ideal day to discuss a holiday or other exciting plans. You may have missed out on a trip at the end of last year and feel ready to book something new. Talk to your friends about a magical getaway together.

Tuesday 28th

Make time for other people and consider encouraging someone younger to crack on with their plans today. Listen to what a close friend has to say and value their personal views or ideas. If someone could benefit from a confidence boost, be the one to step in and say the right thing.

MARCH

· · · · · · · · · · · · · · · · ·

Wednesday 1st

Stay focused and try to achieve a lot at your place of work today. Someone in a position of authority may ask you to take on a more responsible role. Consider whether this is right for you and whether it fits in with your future goals.

Thursday 2nd

Today could prove momentous for your close relationships. If you're looking for love, reach out to others. You might also plan an adventure with your best friends or spend more time with your family.

Friday 3rd

Communication planet Mercury is in your work and health zone, so you might want to line up a meeting to gather the information you're seeking. Try to open doors and discover interesting leads. Today is a good day to learn new things.

Saturday 4th

Consider hanging out with your friends today: the bigger the social gathering the better. There should be a feel-good vibe around your close relationships, and this will refresh and revitalise you. Today is a good day to build stronger bonds with those around you.

Sunday 5th

Make the most of the weekend by spending time with the people you love the most. This is particularly important if things are busy at work, because socialising is a good way to recharge your batteries. It's a great moment to spend time with your optimistic friends.

Monday 6th

It's a great time to think about your emotional security. Be open to life's opportunities and consider experimenting with a new way of working. This might be a good moment to take a break from something that is taking up your time.

Tuesday 7th

Today's full moon is about your work and lifestyle and wanting to get things sorted. People may recognise your skills and talents, and you might have the work-related breakthrough that you need. Alternatively, one job could be coming to an end.

Wednesday 8th

Consider putting new habits and routines in place to boost your wellbeing. This is about quality of life and ensuring that you're fit and healthy in mind, body and soul. A wake-up call could be the reason why you want to take better care of yourself. Prioritise the mind-body-spirit connection.

Thursday 9th

If you've been giving too much recently, or you've taken on a caring role, make sure that you haven't stopped looking after yourself. Caring for other people can be draining, both physically and emotionally. You can't help anyone if you're feeling tired and empty.

Friday 10th

If you've got energy to burn, consider looking into a course of study or a new adventure. You might be thinking about volunteering abroad, either now or in the future. If a family member is asking too much of you, this could be the moment to put your foot down.

Saturday 11th

It's a good day to line up a meeting or interview for next week. If you're looking for work, don't waste any time, as a new job might materialise if you act fast. Consider using your contacts and widening your network.

Sunday 12th

This is a good day to take an active role in your local community. When you take part in an activity that benefits others, this has a positive effect on your life as well. It's important to make time to help those around you.

Monday 13th

You could get pulled up for gossiping or spending too much time socialising at work today. While air signs like Libra love to talk, you should try to stop your desire for friendship from getting in the way of your job. It's important to remain focused on the task at hand.

Tuesday 14th

It's a good day to be inquisitive. Think about exploring new topics and ideas, but be wary of misinformation. Make sure you research things thoroughly, rather than being swept up by the crowd. Open your mind to the world around you.

Wednesday 15th

If you work in a creative or artistic field, this could be very good week. You may be able to lose yourself in your work and make an exciting breakthrough. It's a time when your imagination is at its most vivid. Channel your ideas constructively rather than letting them slip away.

Thursday 16th

If you tend to see the best in people, be careful that you're not being overly gullible. Getting on the wrong side of a person of influence could cost you dearly. Sometimes it's hard to see eye to eye with other people, and this might be one of those days.

Friday 17th

Your ruling planet Venus is in both earth sign Taurus and your finance zone, so it's a good time to focus on money matters and finances in general. Try to recognise the emotional ties that money creates and the importance of prioritising your financial future.

Saturday 18th

Make time to catch up with the ones you love. There should be no subject that's out of bounds, even if someone makes a shocking revelation. Be there with your best ideas and offer to help where possible.

Sunday 19th

If you need to confront an angry individual today, take a step back and try to be the voice of reason and calm. Talk planet Mercury is in your relationship zone this weekend, so it's a good time to have a key conversation with someone close about their behaviour.

Monday 20th

Close connections will be important right now, as the Sun enters Aries and your relationship zone today. Things could happen quickly when it comes to love, and one of you might leap in feet first. Feel your emotions fully and act spontaneously in affairs of the heart. New beginnings are on the way.

Tuesday 21st

Certain areas of your life are moving forward now, possibly at a fast pace. Today's new moon is a good opportunity to state your intentions and start afresh. If you're looking for love, this new moon is great for taking the initiative and acting decisively.

Wednesday 22nd

This isn't the time to be indecisive in love. Instead, your stars are encouraging you to be proactive in your close relationships and to be decisive. It's a good moment to make up your mind. Being around other people who are bold and courageous can rub off on you in a good way.

Thursday 23rd

Take a closer look at what you do in life that brings you enjoyment. Notice when you feel disappointed or out of control. If the balance of power is out within a relationship, now's the time to consider what you can do about it.

Friday 24th

Your ruling planet Venus remains steady in Taurus, and this turns the spotlight towards the shared resources in your life. Teamwork may prove helpful, as will a decision to rely on someone close. Work with other people to boost your sense of security. Be open to the unexpected.

Saturday 25th

Action planet Mars moves into star sign Cancer today, switching on your ambition. This is your career and vocation zone, and Mars remains here until May 20th. Focus on these key areas of your life and consider your next steps. Take another person's lead and renew your sense of direction.

Sunday 26th

If you want to revitalise a close relationship, it's a good idea to do something different today. Get away from your everyday environment and embrace an adventure. Get to know your partner or someone close on a deeper level.

Monday 27th

It looks as if there's a lot to talk about at the moment, so you might be finding out all kinds of information about someone new. It's a good day to learn a language or be around people you wouldn't normally hang out with. Push back the boundaries of convention and live life on the edge.

Tuesday 28th

It's a perfect day for compliments, kind gestures and being open-hearted. This could go both ways, whether you're the one who gives or receives a confidence boost. Your relationships are a precious resource and should be treated as such.

Wednesday 29th

Today is great for coming up with new ideas about how to pursue the career of your choice. Step outside of your comfort zone and use lateral thinking to boost your clever mind. You might be offered a promotion soon.

Thursday 30th

Today's stars might bring a surprise or coincide with an unexpected gift. Alternatively, someone you rely on may withdraw their support. Hopefully the outcome is positive, but be prepared to take swift action.

Friday 31st

If you've not spent much time with your friends recently, line up a social get-together today or tomorrow. The moon is in your friendship and group zone, so being around other people will boost your spirits. If you're typical of your star sign, you don't like to spend too much time alone.

APRIL

. . . .

Saturday 1st

Try to avoid difficult conversations with the people closest to you if you want the weekend to go smoothly. Friendship and love often go hand in hand, so spend some quality time with someone special today.

Sunday 2nd

If you're feeling tired or low on energy today, take some time out to be by yourself. Catch up on your sleep or have a lazy day. Switching off could turn into a creative venture as it allows space for your imagination to thrive. Follow up on a work idea this evening.

Monday 3rd

This is a key week to discuss money and sort things out with people close to you. Talk planet Mercury will be in your finance zone for the next couple of months. It's a good time to get your financial ducks in a row, so think about seeking expert advice.

Tuesday 4th

You may not have much incentive to work today and might therefore spend more time staring out the window than getting things done. Pace yourself if you're feeling tired. Be aware that your dreams could be extra lively and your quality of sleep worse than usual.

Wednesday 5th

Tonight's full moon falls in your star sign, and could signify the completion or culmination of something. You may hear important news or be the recipient of an award, a compliment or an acknowledgement. It's your time to shine.

Thursday 6th

If you're a typical Libra, you may often find it hard to be decisive. However, this week's full moon requires your attention. This is especially true concerning a relationship, either personal or professional. Now could be a turning point regarding your love life, so express your true self and be honest.

Friday 7th

Full moons heighten emotions and urge you to bring things out into the open. Talk to the people closest to you about your wants and needs, and don't ignore your feelings. This evening has a wonderfully romantic vibe. You and someone close could connect on a deeper level.

Saturday 8th

This is a good day to reach out to someone you don't see eye to eye with. Initiate a conversation with a competitor or rival; you could quickly discover that you're reading from the same page. The more energy you put into something, the faster you can make progress.

Sunday 9th

You may have to agree to disagree with someone close first thing in the morning. Try not to let a minor issue turn into a major problem. It's important to find someone you can talk to who sees your side of things.

Monday 10th

Keep things light today and try not to worry about the more serious issues of life. Ideally, you want to be around people who have a positive outlook and know how to make you smile. Laughter can be a welcome tonic, so point yourself in the direction of fun and games.

Tuesday 11th

Things should begin to ease for you today as your planet Venus enters Gemini, lighting up the horoscope zone where you find meaning in life. The more you broaden your horizons, the more fulfilled you will feel. A third party could open the door to a travel or study adventure.

Wednesday 12th

Luck and love often go hand in hand, and someone close to you may give you a reason to celebrate today. If you can work from home today, this might be preferable. Take a risk and make a well-calculated move that could help you moving forward.

Thursday 13th

If someone in your family doesn't see eye to eye with you when it comes to love and relationships, it might be best to keep your distance today. If you need a project to lose yourself in, look for a creative obsession that grabs your attention. Channel your passion into art or a hobby.

Friday 14th

Remain curious about life and all that it has to offer. You may want to learn something new, or you might discover a missing piece of information. Refresh, renew and revive yourself. Stay engaged and keep exploring the world around you.

Saturday 15th

It's an excellent day for romance and meeting your match. Dating apps are an exciting way of boosting your chances of romance. If you're a parent, spend quality time with your child, especially if they have big news.

Sunday 16th

Sunday is traditionally a day of rest, but you might be working or catching up on a time-consuming project. Even if you're feeling tired, it's worth putting in some extra time and effort so that you're ready for the week ahead. The planet of ambition is boosting your career zone, so make the most of it.

Monday 17th

It's important that you have a job that fulfils you emotionally. As a Libra, any activity that allows you to tap into your creativity or access your caring nature is ideal. The more you encourage your imaginative nature, the better.

Tuesday 18th

Turn your attention towards your close relationships. A powerful new eclipse cycle begins this week, and for you this is about love and partnerships. Eclipses represent accelerated growth, so events may happen quickly. Be open to love and aim to recalibrate the work/life balance.

Wednesday 19th

Lucky Jupiter is involved in this week's eclipse astrology, so you might feel both passionate and dramatic. There could be lots of excitement coming your way, perhaps in the form of a special gift from someone close. If you meet someone new, this could have a positive impact on your life.

Thursday 20th

Today's solar eclipse represents a massive energy boost in your relationship zone, and this could prove to be a huge turning point in your life. Eclipses represent change, so you're likely to meet someone new or break free from a negative situation. It depends on your circumstances.

Friday 21st

Talk planet Mercury turns retrograde in your finance zone, and this means that you may have to play a waiting game until mid-May when it comes to money. Try not to take any unnecessary risks, and make sure you're well-informed.

Saturday 22nd

You may have to overcome a stumbling block if you want to book a holiday or course, perhaps related to a work or home issue. Try not to let fear hold you back, but at the same time be realistic about what you can and can't achieve.

Sunday 23rd

Love could save the day if your other half steps in to suggest a solution to an issue that's been bothering you. Keep the lines of communication wide open and talk through all the possibilities. You may have to try harder than usual to get what you want today.

Monday 24th

Someone may go back on their word today, which might leave you feeling frustrated. Don't give up, and instead push for the solution that you need. An old contact or work colleague might get back in touch with you.

Tuesday 25th

It's an excellent day to appeal to a boss or a person in authority. Use your charm and persuasive abilities to get on the right side of other people to boost your chances of success.

Wednesday 26th

The moon remains in your career zone, so it might be worth pushing that little bit harder to impress others today. If you're busy with a project or deadline, you may have to prioritise your work over your relationships.

Thursday 27th

If you're typical of your star sign, you love socialising and making friends. You may be keen to expand your social circle today, but don't go over the top trying to please everyone. Some secrets are best kept to yourself. Keep friendships light and avoid any taboo areas.

Friday 28th

Don't allow other people to pressure you into spending too much money. This doesn't mean you can't still enjoy yourself, but keep a close eye on your finances. Try not to compare yourself to others. You might face challenges at work today.

Saturday 29th

Being around the right people can make a big difference to your mood. Hang out with loved ones who boost your sense of wellbeing and lift your spirits. It's worth going all out to grab a job that has your name written all over it. Consider sending a spontaneous job application.

Sunday 30th

Take a step back today and slow things down. Have a lie-in or keep your day free to chill and relax. You may need to come up with some new ideas for a future project. Give yourself the time and space to allow your creative imagination free rein.

MAY

. . . .

Monday 1st

Your stars suggest that an old problem will come to the fore today. However, this might not be the best time to revisit the issue. Instead, let go of what's not working, close the door and move on. A late-night conversation about money could be revelatory if approached correctly.

Tuesday 2nd

With the moon in your star sign today, your caring nature will be on show. Kindness is one of your key qualities, so make a point of smiling at other people and try to be open and giving. It rarely takes a lot to make someone else feel better.

Wednesday 3rd

Make sure that you're not taken advantage of at work. You may have a giving nature, but that doesn't mean you have to bend over backwards to keep your boss happy. Rather than work late at the office, consider standing up for yourself and speaking your mind. Stay calm and focused.

Thursday 4th

You may feel disillusioned or dissatisfied today. Know that this is temporary. There are ways to ensure you feel more grounded, and earthy activities are a great way to relieve pressure. Try walking, gardening, cooking, making things, or any activity that keeps you steady.

Friday 5th

Today's lunar eclipse may mean that you need to deal with an inheritance, mortgage or loan. It's via your past and the people closest to you where security can be found. This is a powerful eclipse that will shed light on your values.

Saturday 6th

Eclipses often coincide with the highs and lows of life. If unexpected expenses crop up today or you hear about a financial loss, consider taking your time before responding. It may be that once things settle in a few days, you'll be more able to come up with a clever solution to a current challenge.

Sunday 7th

Your planet Venus moves star sign today. Over the next few weeks, try and restore a sense of harmony at work and get life back on track. Your Libra skills, such as diplomacy and mediation, will be in demand, and this could be your opportunity to shine.

Monday 8th

Continue a conversation that you started over the weekend. If this sets you on a new path or provides the chance to gain new qualifications, you're on the right track. It's a good day for reaching out to your relatives and neighbours, especially someone you haven't seen in a while.

Tuesday 9th

Don't take money matters for granted: the wheel of fortune turns rapidly and things could happen quickly today. Keep one step ahead and think about new ways of making money. Consider learning more about new technologies.

Wednesday 10th

It may be time to bring your mediating skills to the boardroom or the office. If you're in contact with someone angry and difficult to be around, find ways to avoid their bad behaviour. For example, you could work from home.

Thursday 11th

If you're confronted with either an emotional or a financial problem, resolve to deal with the situation today. Doing so might lead to an argument, but sometimes it's better to speak up than to remain silent. By choosing to say nothing, you could actually make things worse.

Friday 12th

Consider giving yourself the weekend to think things through when it comes to money or a financial issue. You may have more information to hand that helps you deal with a matter directly by the start of next week. For now, do your research and explore all your options.

Saturday 13th

Get the right people on your side this weekend. Look to your colleagues for support and inspiration. This is particularly important if you're trying to implement significant changes at your place of work. The bigger your team, the greater your chances of success.

Sunday 14th

It may be the weekend, but the spotlight is on your work and routine, so you might be busy getting creative with a work project or improving your fitness levels. Boost your mental faculties and ensure you're working at optimum performance. It's not a good day for lazing around.

Monday 15th

Talk planet Mercury turns direct today, and this may coincide with news about a personal money matter. Think about seeking out someone new who complements your skills. It's an ideal day to get expert advice regarding your work.

Tuesday 16th

You might meet a new business partner today or find the person you've been looking for to help you with a personal goal. It's an ideal time to go with the flow, so try to use visualisation to attract abundance into your life.

Wednesday 17th

Look out for a new opportunity to earn money and improve your financial situation. Anything that begins when lucky Jupiter is powerful has the potential to be successful. You could receive an inheritance, benefit from an investment or finalise a new business partnership.

Thursday 18th

Try to eliminate debt from your life and look at ways of using your money to good effect. Get good financial advice and have a system in place so you know what's coming in and what's going out of your money pot.

. . . .

Friday 19th

Today's new moon falls in Taurus and in one of the money zones in your horoscope. A new moon is an ideal time to wipe the slate clean and start afresh. At the very least, it's an excellent time to set your intentions moving forward. Turn over a new leaf.

Saturday 20th

Friends and family could be the source of entertainment or drama now and over the next six weeks. Inject some fresh energy into your friendships and group activities. It's an ideal time to consider joining a new club, group or society.

Sunday 21st

It's not the best day to get involved in a heated debate with those closest to you, as tempers could flare quickly. Avoid these conversations as best you can and be around the people in your life who know how to enjoy the good times.

Monday 22nd

You should be able to spend less time focused on a money matter or financial issue from this week onwards. Focus on being sociable and draw up new plans for adventure. Get together with a group of your best friends and talk about holidays and educational goals.

Tuesday 23rd

Move beyond your comfort zone and say yes to a new experience, as this is where fulfilment lies. Listen out for a new opportunity or idea that comes your way and engage actively with life. Trust your luck and take a risk.

Wednesday 24th

You might have some tough decisions to make about where your money goes and what you spend it on. This could be the right time to put a stop to something that's been an unnecessary drain on your income.

Thursday 25th

The moon is in your friendship zone, so it's a great day to reach out to other people. If you're a typical Libra, you enjoy creating new partnerships in your life. Team up with someone new and become a double act.

Friday 26th

Today is not about what you know, it's who you know, so work those connections. This could turn out to be a socially active time for you in which you meet new friends or find out about new groups to join.

Saturday 27th

Just because it's a long weekend doesn't mean you have to go into overdrive and line up a big adventure. It might do you the world of good to cancel your plans and spend more time at home. The cosmos is giving you permission to put your feet up and take it easy.

Sunday 28th

If you start to sink into a bad mood today, it's probably a good idea to get out and go somewhere different. Even a few hours away from your normal environment could lift your spirits. It's a good idea to stay off social media, especially if you don't want to find out what your friends are up to.

Monday 29th

Take your time and slow down the pace this bank holiday Monday. You're allowed to have an afternoon nap or binge-watch your favourite TV programme without feeling guilty. The moon's move back into your star sign in the late afternoon should bring a welcome energy boost.

Tuesday 30th

Being in the world may be just the tonic you need. If you've been feeling unwell or overly tired, hopefully the long weekend has rejuvenated your spirits. You're one of the air signs, which means you're likely to be a social animal and at your best when you're connecting with your fellow human beings.

Wednesday 31st

You may find it hard to get back into the swing of work or other responsibilities today. Be accepting of this and allow yourself small treats throughout the day. This might be as simple as going for a walk. Care for yourself first.

JUNE
······················

Thursday 1st
Money matters may require careful handling over the next few days. You could receive a windfall, or unexpected expenses might crop up. You currently have the entrepreneurial planets in your money zone, so make the most of this.

Friday 2nd
Be wary in your financial partnerships, both personal and professional. You might discover that someone close can't afford what you're planning together, or you may be disappointed to discover that your return on an investment or loan was way lower than you expected.

Saturday 3rd
You might be making plans and looking ahead to what comes next in your life. It's a good time to do so, because this weekend's full moon triggers your travel zone. Even if you don't have the freedom you crave, you still need an activity to lose yourself in, whether it's academic or philosophical.

Sunday 4th
Focus on the bigger picture today and consider booking a holiday or a workshop. Keep your eye on the ball when it comes to money matters, and listen out for a brilliant idea that could help you resolve an important issue.

Monday 5th

Your planet Venus moves into fire sign Leo today. Use your connections and trust your intuition when it comes to your friends. When you're around people who lift your mood, you will feel a greater sense of self-worth; when you're around a person with toxic energy, the opposite happens.

Tuesday 6th

Work alongside your family or the people you live with today, whether you're sharing expenses or resources. Think about making a financial spreadsheet to give you a better idea of what you're spending. This could be especially helpful if you're planning for an anniversary or a special event.

Wednesday 7th

If one relationship in your life is unusually intense, you might need to take a step back to create some distance and get a fresh perspective on what's happening. Try and keep your emotions in check and deal with this situation logically and rationally.

Thursday 8th

You may have to back out of a deal if it's proving too expensive or you're too emotionally attached. Notice who triggers your emotions and when and where you're becoming overly obsessive about a situation. This might be linked to love, parenting or a hobby.

Friday 9th

Don't get sucked into a work situation that leaves you unable to get away or take a break. If you're typical of your star sign, you don't like to upset other people; however, it's important to ensure your needs are being met. Pleasing others ahead of yourself is sure to leave you feeling exhausted.

Saturday 10th

Your stars may flag up an issue from the past, and you might realise that you want to cut ties and move away from a situation that no longer works for you. You may need to act drastically if doing so means you can move on from a situation that's not helping you emotionally or psychologically.

Sunday 11th

If you want to change external events, start by working on your inner self. The changes within will trigger the changes you desire out in the world. There may be an opportunity to return to your past: someone from your childhood could be in touch, or you might return to a place you once lived.

Monday 12th

It's a good time to turn to your friends, especially if you're trying to make sense of recent events. The people who know you best will be able to give you an alternative perspective on what's going on. Ask the person closest to you for some honest advice or guidance.

Tuesday 13th

If you're keen to get away on a last-minute trip or travel opportunity, aim for Sunday 18th, as this is when there will be a new moon in your travel zone. Rather than going away on your own, think about planning an adventure with the people in your life that you love most.

Wednesday 14th

You may need a little bit of good fortune now if you're going to be able to afford an exciting event that's coming along soon. The good news is that you have luck on your side. Find the right person to give you the advice you're seeking.

Thursday 15th

Don't let fear or doubt stop you from living your life to the fullest. Try to remove any obstacles and consider travelling or joining your friends on a big adventure. Work might be the only thing holding you back, but even then, you may be able to find a solution.

Friday 16th

If you're out of work or unemployed, consider your options moving forward. A new opportunity could arise to help you in an unexpected way. Keep talking about what's possible and ask for other people's ideas and advice.

Saturday 17th

If you're aware that you have a problem saying no and you're unable to set healthy boundaries at work, it's time to reassess your situation. If you're the one who's constantly working the weekend shift or taking on extra responsibility, you could try being more assertive and standing your ground.

Sunday 18th

Today's new moon falls in Gemini and in your travel and study zone, and this will give you the impetus to start something new. You might be signing up for a course or be thinking about where you want to travel in the future. This is a great opportunity to make some long-term plans.

Monday 19th

The planetary flow is calling you out into the world. This is not the time to be overly cautious or hold back. Instead, try to move beyond your comfort zone and say yes to a new or different experience.

Tuesday 20th

If you receive news of a successful work application, promotion or pay rise, it may take a while for this to sink in. Perhaps you're being cautiously optimistic. Understand your limitations, but be prepared to take a necessary risk if it will help you to achieve success.

Wednesday 21st

This could be a pivotal week, especially regarding the future of your career or vocation. Look out for a signpost that points you in the right direction. If you already know this is likely to be a key period for your working life, get ready. The Sun moves into your career zone and encourages you to shine.

Thursday 22nd

It's a good day for social events and joining in with your friends, so don't let anything hold you back from enjoying yourself. Perhaps there's a romantic reason to go out and socialise. If you've fallen for a friend, this might be the moment to let them know.

Friday 23rd

Try not to schedule anything important today. You may be feeling tired if you were out on the town last night, or perhaps your energy levels have peaked and you're ready for the weekend. That doesn't mean you can't impress the boss, but be careful not to get carried away.

. . . .

Saturday 24th

You may be seeking your escape from the everyday world this weekend. This is a fertile time for dreams and imagination, so try to create some space in your life to allow your creative source to rise to the surface. Be discerning and questioning around new ideas.

Sunday 25th

Neptune's realm is one of fantasy, so don't lose yourself entirely today. Keep your feet on the ground and engage your logical and rational brain. Some ideas aren't worth following, and some promises may not be kept.

Monday 26th

Today's planetary clash between Mars and Uranus is volatile. It's a great time to be a rebel with a cause, but not so great for getting involved in a fiery argument. Try not to be a daredevil and don't leap spontaneously into a friend's drama.

Tuesday 27th

Talk planet Mercury moves into your career and vocation zone today. This means that the next two weeks are a brilliant time for interviews, meetings and sending job applications. Make sure you follow up on any new ideas.

Wednesday 28th

The moon is in your star sign for the next couple of days, so use this cosmic nudge to make the first move when it comes to finding work or pitching for a promotion. You're likely to have a way with words, so take this opportunity to talk yourself into a better position.

Thursday 29th

If you struggle with commitment, it's important to take
a closer look at the reasons for this. This is particularly
important when it comes to your employment. If you remain
indecisive or keep changing your mind, you might leave it too
late to get the job that you desire.

Friday 30th

Be honest with yourself: if you're worried about committing to
a role or position, it might be because you believe you might
miss out on something better. Life is calling you to stick to
one path and do whatever it takes to prove your loyalty and
reliability. A period of hard work beckons.

JULY

· · · · · · · · · · · · · · · · ·

Saturday 1st

This might turn out to be a lucky weekend if you find yourself in the right place at the right time. Good timing and good luck may bring a new opportunity your way. Your enthusiasm and self-belief are the added ingredients that will bring you success.

Sunday 2nd

You may want to celebrate with friends or family today. However, your plans could change suddenly, and one friend might let you down. It's not the best day to mix love and friendship. A spontaneous move could backfire on you.

Monday 3rd

Today's full moon cuts across the foundations of your horoscope. You should see clearly where you've come from, how you've developed and where this has led you to. You might be struggling to juggle work and home life. Use the light of the full moon to make a clear and insightful decision.

Tuesday 4th

Listen to your intuition and trust yourself. The month's full moon phase is often an emotional time in which your dreams are more revealing than usual. You may be pulled back into the past or the family fold. Ensure that you keep moving forward and try not to take a backwards step.

Wednesday 5th

You may come to the realisation that what you want to do in life is going to be too expensive. This might be linked to parenting, a hobby or your dream vocation in life. If you're going to ask for support today, choose your friends carefully.

Thursday 6th

When it comes to love, what you want when and what someone else wants might be miles apart. Be honest in your romantic relationships and make sure it's clear what you're both interested in. A shared understanding is the key to a supportive partnership.

Friday 7th

Your stars spell good news for work and money matters today. Consider taking advantage of any news or information that comes your way first thing this morning. Gather information quickly, and act if you need to.

Saturday 8th

It's important to look after yourself and put your needs first. If you've been spending too much time and energy caring for others, adjust the balance. Always begin by helping yourself before helping others. It's a perfect day for finding your flow and indulging in an artistic activity.

Sunday 9th

If your dreams and imagination inspire you, follow them.
Your ambition may benefit from some extra stimulation today,
so consider turning to a favourite author or diving into a
movie. Try not to let reality kick in, and instead allow your
imagination to take you away.

Monday 10th

Action planet Mars leaves sociable Leo and enters quieter Virgo
today. This indicates a change of pace, whether you want more
time to yourself or you're slowing down for another reason.
As Mars is your partner planet, this may be about the one you
love, perhaps regarding their work situation.

Tuesday 11th

If you're a typical Libra, you'll find it hard to stay away from
the action, even if your priorities are changing. You still
need friends and group activities in your life to keep you
entertained, so find your place within your social circle and
make sure you can play your part.

Wednesday 12th

Turn your attention towards work and money matters. It's
easy to let these key areas of your life slide if you're caught up
with personal affairs. Your star sign is all about relationships,
but it's important that you work on all your partnerships,
including the ones that help you to prosper financially.

Thursday 13th

The wheel of fortune is shifting, and the areas of major change in your life may now be linked more to relationships than to money matters. Give some thought to your close relationships moving forward, especially if someone isn't happy or feels that they need more attention.

Friday 14th

This is a good time to be in the public eye and to engage with people of influence, so networking might be the best way to improve your prospects. You may find that you're busy and popular at work right now. Keeping on the right side of other people is a wise move in all areas.

Saturday 15th

You may not be able to keep the whole weekend clear of work, but do your best to take a break. If you can, get away from it all today and go somewhere completely different; if one of your best friends is by your side on your adventure, even better. Seize the day.

Sunday 16th

The day before the new moon is ideal for rest and retreat. Gather your energy and be ready to start something fresh once the new moon phase kicks in. This is an important time to reset your compass and look to the future. The right move could help to secure your financial situation.

Monday 17th

Today's new moon highlights your career and vocation zone. This may be the right time to make a big decision regarding your work and future path, as you should have more of a sense of what needs to happen, where you're heading and why. Initiate a fresh start and open a new door.

Tuesday 18th

It may have become obvious that something is preventing you from achieving your work or career goals. Alternatively, you might not be immediately aware of an attachment to the past or a family issue that is holding you back. This would be a good time to delve a little deeper on a psychological level.

Wednesday 19th

Make time for your friends and catch up with someone you haven't seen for a while, as doing so could benefit both of you on different levels. An act of generosity should be well-received now. Your friend might know exactly what to say to help you decide what to do next.

Thursday 20th

You may be feeling unusually frustrated now, especially if someone in your life is holding you back. You might be feeling the excitement slipping away, either yours or someone else's, or you may have more serious concerns that need addressing.

Friday 21st

It's not a good idea to channel your anger inward. Make sure you express what you're feeling, even if it means confronting a difficult situation in your life. Be kinder to yourself, and try to identify and acknowledge where any blame lies. Consider cutting ties and be courageous in moving on.

Saturday 22nd

You might be dealing with emotional baggage, but it is often better to be free of the past. Now is a good time to move away from a toxic situation, so aim to declutter, release and let go. Consider using this period to clear away what's old and create space for new energy to come in.

Sunday 23rd

Your planet Venus turns retrograde in your friendship and group zone today. This may prove significant in a friendship or a personal relationship. Notice if someone close has a change of heart. Alternatively, you may find that you're the one at a key turning point in life.

Monday 24th

This could be an ideal time to release and let go. Your friendships may be shifting, or you might be ready to move away from a group activity that consumes your time and energy. When you have the right people by your side, your skills and talents shine brightest.

Tuesday 25th

If you have an important role to play within a group of people in your life today, make sure that you've taken on this role because you want to, not because you feel obliged to. From now up until early September, try to explore your friendships on a deeper level.

Wednesday 26th

Take a look at your values and self-worth today. If you're attached to your earnings or believe that you're worthy only because of what you own, try to understand that this isn't a true reflection of who you are. The more you learn to love yourself for your inner qualities, the more fulfilling your life experience will be.

Thursday 27th

It's possible that a new relationship will emerge today, or that you will have a profound experience with a friend that causes you to recognise that your feelings for one another are changing. This isn't the time to make a major decision regarding your love life. However, don't let this stop you from exploring a relationship further.

Friday 28th

If you're a typical Libra, you're sociable by nature. There's a possibility, however, that you're veering away from a friendship group, perhaps because you want to spend less time around other people. If your busy life doesn't allow you any time for introspection or spiritual solace, shift the balance.

Saturday 29th

This is an ideal weekend to start journalling or to commit to a course of study. Whether you're discovering new ideas or working on personal development, do whatever's necessary to become the best person you can be. Consider this period a key time of inner preparation.

Sunday 30th

It's an ideal Sunday to learn more about the things you believe, either through meditation or study. You may want something more from life than work and socialising now. Seek a deeper resonance within yourself.

Monday 31st

There may be an opportunity to return to your past today. Someone you knew growing up could get back in touch with you, or perhaps a family member initiates a trip down memory lane. Accept a chance to embrace your past, as this is where hidden riches can sometimes be found.

AUGUST

....

Tuesday 1st

A full moon period is a time of celebration, and today this also means that it's a good time to arrange a get-together with a beloved friend. If you're looking for a big break at work, use your network of friends and connections to make progress.

Wednesday 2nd

You may be in a situation where you can help other people, especially if you feel a sense of responsibility or duty to look after those around you. Don't allow negative emotions to kick in, and instead remember to be kind to yourself.

Thursday 3rd

Other people may require your time and attention now, so caring for yourself and others could prove to be a dominant theme today. Take time out when you can this week to avoid overloading your schedule. You may need more time alone to rest and retreat.

Friday 4th

You might be ready for a break after a busy period, or perhaps you're back from a holiday and are getting used to your daily schedule. You're wise to do more of the sensible stuff now. Pay close attention to your work, routine and lifestyle.

Saturday 5th

Give yourself up to love while the moon is in both passionate Aries and your relationship zone this weekend. Shut the door on the world and enjoy some time with your other half or someone new. It's too easy to get caught up with life and lose track of your relationship.

Sunday 6th

Work to recalibrate your close relationships. Your star sign tends not to like conflict, but that doesn't mean you shouldn't ask for what you want. If something is missing in a significant relationship or a key friendship in your life, be direct and honest with the person concerned.

Monday 7th

It's a good week to resolve an issue in your life so that you can put bad feelings behind you and get back to a situation that's more peaceful and harmonious. If someone's not worth your time and effort, let them know.

Tuesday 8th

Don't fight your feelings today. The moon is in your intimacy zone, so it's a time when emotions could be intense. You may want to leap in spontaneously and prove your passion. Live life to the fullest.

Wednesday 9th

Plans could change suddenly today. Consider prioritising the social side of life, as this is where fun can be found. If you've been burning the candle at both ends recently, you might have to let down a good friend. Do whatever feels right for you.

. . . .

Thursday 10th

It's a good idea to focus on your health and wellbeing today. There may be a family relationship you want to heal, but you also need to think carefully about whether this is the right time to do so. You need to have inner strength before reaching out to someone close. A gift from your past has the potential to brighten your day.

Friday 11th

If you feel like you're being pulled in different directions, you'll be ready for the weekend. A conversation might catches you off-guard and could go on for hours. If you're trying to get work done or you're busy, expect more interruptions than usual.

Saturday 12th

If you didn't get much done yesterday, you might be keen to make amends and catch up on your work today. There's a productive feel to your stars, whether you're training for a marathon or completing a work deadline. A solo project might be the best fit to help you concentrate.

Sunday 13th

It's a good day to reach out to an influential friend. If you know there's someone who can help you with a personal goal, you should think about making a connection. If you're interested in finding love, ask your friends for an introduction and make a commitment to being more sociable.

Monday 14th

A crisis or drama at home could disrupt your work plans first thing, but don't feel bad if you need to prioritise your family life. Your friends might call you more over the next couple of days. Fill your day with fun and laughter.

Tuesday 15th

It may be hard to get into a work mindset this week. The sociable side of your nature is being called forth, so you will be more interested in discussing fun ideas and plans. This evening, be around the person or group of people who make you laugh uncontrollably.

Wednesday 16th

Today's new moon in sociable Leo is ideal for a mid-week event with friends. Remember that face-to-face connections are often more rewarding than meetings online. It's not a good day to splash out on new technology.

Thursday 17th

Work deadlines might catch up with you now, especially if you've been relatively slack in the first half of the week. Shut the door on any noise and try and create a quiet space to concentrate and get things done. It's not the most exciting day, so focus on completing your to-do list.

Friday 18th

What would benefit you now? More rest? More research? More planning? Do whatever feels right for you and aim for a slower pace of life. You will benefit from time to yourself now, so listen to your inner voice and be thoughtful, quiet and still.

. . . .

Saturday 19th

Don't feel you have to make a snap decision today if you're not ready. Be reflective and actively engage in thinking through your next steps. Ease your way into the weekend with a long lie-in or a leisurely breakfast. This afternoon is an ideal time to work on a personal goal.

Sunday 20th

The moon is in Libra, so it's a good time to consider your image and how you come across to other people. What fulfils you emotionally? Spend some quality time today engaging with your skills and talents, especially if you've been neglecting a hobby or passion of late.

Monday 21st

It's a great time to showcase your talents and show off your natural charisma. It's a good day to impress other people, and you should find that you're the centre of attention wherever you go. By the evening you may feel exhausted and decide to have an early night.

Tuesday 22nd

Use your connections and trust your intuition when it comes to other people. A love relationship or close partnership in your life could unsettle you without an explanation. There's a theme of mistrust in the air, so beware of being led astray. It could be up to you to put things right.

Wednesday 23rd

When communication planet Mercury turns retrograde and dives deep into the most hidden zone of your horoscope, what happens behind the scenes is as important as what's visible. Listen to your inner voice and try not to dismiss unconscious thoughts. Slow things down.

Thursday 24th

Keep the lines of communication open today and seek advice or support from other people. This is especially important if you're feeling out of sorts or you're unsure about what's happening in a close relationship. Don't try to force yourself to do anything. Let things be.

Friday 25th

It's a great day for getting things done, especially regarding a family matter. You will feel supported if a partner in your life takes charge and helps you make steady progress. Delve back into the past, sort things out and declutter.

Saturday 26th

You may have an insight today about where you need to let go or bring something in your life to completion. This might be around work, your lifestyle or your fitness. Be realistic about what you can achieve, close the door on what's not working out and get ready to start afresh.

Sunday 27th

Life is beginning to shift and change for the better as action planet Mars, which represents ambition and drive, enters your star sign today. This is good news if you're looking to be proactive, as it could help you to get things done. Be more forthright and honest in your interactions.

Monday 28th

It can be exhausting if you're looking after an elderly parent, or if you have a lot of responsibility at home. Try not to overdo the caring aspect in your life, otherwise you could be heading for a burnout. Look for help and support within your family.

Tuesday 29th

Take a step back from digital media and try a different approach. You might find it difficult to keep up a relationship if your only form of contact is online. Keep close tabs on money. Unexpected expenses or a switch in earnings may require your attention. Be flexible and adaptable.

Wednesday 30th

Now's the time to consider taking things seriously, especially when it comes to your working life. Improve your discipline levels or commit to a healthy habit. Don't ignore any warning signs and be thorough in your attention to detail. It's an ideal full moon to give up a bad habit.

Thursday 31st

Today's full moon highlights your work and how you can be of help to others, but don't get pulled into other people's dramas. Take on too much and you could quickly find yourself feeling overwhelmed. A good cry could be the tonic you need.

SEPTEMBER

· · · · · · · · · · · · · · · · ·

Friday 1st

You may feel emotional first thing this morning, perhaps as a result of something that's happening at work. Let your emotions flow and be aware that this might be a sensitive time for you. Be aware that you could easily overreact to someone who's being angry or loud.

Saturday 2nd

The moon is in your relationship zone all weekend, and this means that it's a good time to engage with your close relationships, especially as Venus, the planet of love, turns direct on Monday 4th. You may want to review the events of past six weeks, since Venus turned retrograde on July 23rd.

Sunday 3rd

If you don't want to be around your partner's family today, it's okay to say so. If your family are getting involved in your love life in a detrimental way, it might be best to tell them to keep out of the way. Sometimes you have to be resolute if your needs are to be met. Be bold and stand your ground.

Monday 4th

Your planet Venus turns direct today, and this may spell good news for your love life. Notice who contacts you or comes into your life now, especially if you hear from someone from your past. Allow yourself to get excited and feel positive.

Tuesday 5th

You might be tempted to rush in and make a spontaneous move today, especially if you've recently found out what someone else thinks about you. However, there may be a lot more to discover or mull over yet. What's most important is that you know your own mind.

Wednesday 6th

The planet of communication Mercury is quiet this week and continues to move backwards in the most hidden zone of your horoscope. This is where inner work takes place, and means that it's time to slow down, take a step back and look at your life from a fresh perspective.

Thursday 7th

It would be easy to feel scared if you take in too much information now. Once you start searching on the internet, you can lose yourself down a rabbit hole of conflicting opinions. You should try to take a break from technology today.

Friday 8th

Listen to your inner voice and watch out for any signposts that signal freedom. You should have a strong sense that your moral compass is guiding you, and this could lead you to help another person or join in with a fundraising or charity venture.

Saturday 9th

If you're typical of your star sign, it's likely to be important that you work for a company that has strong ethics and a sound moral code. Look out for an opportunity to further the charitable aspect of your work today.

Sunday 10th

It may be the weekend, but the moon is shining bright in your career zone. You may be playing a key role in a work event or spending time working on your own projects or business. Chill out this evening so that you're ready and refreshed for the week ahead.

Monday 11th

If you've recently helped a friend with an emotional issue, today might be the day that they repay the favour. Love is in the ascendancy, so you may recognise that your feelings for a friend are getting stronger day by day.

Tuesday 12th

If you have a generous nature, you may sometimes receive gifts or compliments. However, it's important that people don't take advantage of your trusting nature. It might be wise to look after yourself today.

Wednesday 13th

You might need to slow things down, especially if you feel weighed down by a heavy workload that's proving stressful. Learn from the lessons you've gained recently and prioritise your wellbeing whenever possible. Aim to have a routine in place that works for you.

Thursday 14th

You could be discussing money or an important issue with people at home today. Make sure that conversations are open and honest and seek expert advice where necessary. Don't rush in if you don't have all the information.

Friday 15th

Take some time out for yourself during the new moon phase this weekend. If you're worried about your work, being quiet will help to still any anxiety. As one of the air signs, you might often let your mind run away with you. You can learn a lot from inner wisdom and quiet contemplation.

Saturday 16th

One of the benefits of spending time alone is that it allows creative ideas to come to you naturally. Whether your creative place is in the shower, on a walk or in the garden, spend time this weekend reconnecting with nature and encouraging your inner voice to be heard.

Sunday 17th

It's a perfect day for being overly indulgent and enjoying yourself with your friends or loved ones. Consider splashing out and treating someone special, especially if you're celebrating a birthday or special anniversary. Other people may look to you to take the lead at a social event.

Monday 18th

Start the week as you mean to go on by being at your most professional and ambitious. Dress for success and show other people that you mean business. When you put your mind to it, you can pursue your passions wholeheartedly. Keep focused and make a good impression.

Tuesday 19th

You may be susceptible to confusion or seduction today, so keep your feet firmly on the ground. Pay attention to the facts and try to discern what's true and what's not. You need a firm anchor in life so that you don't drift or lose yourself. Find your escape without compromising your integrity.

Wednesday 20th

You might find yourself feeling quite jumpy today, so steer clear of anything spooky. Try not to be overly superstitious or make too much of a coincidence. It might help to talk things through with someone whose opinion you trust this evening.

Thursday 21st

You may feel closely connected to your ancestors or the people you knew well who are no longer with us. Spend some time remembering them and share those memories with the people closest to you. Doing so should help bring about a sense of closure that helps you shut the door on the past.

Friday 22nd

You should feel more willing to explore the spiritual side of life today. This is a pivotal time in the year when one season is coming to an end and a new season is about to begin, and this energy will be particularly important for you now.

Saturday 23rd

The Sun's move into your star sign heralds the equinox, where day and night are of equal lengths. It's an ideal time to regain balance in your life and seek harmony both at home and within your close relationships. This could be the moment to have the conversation you've been putting off for some time.

Sunday 24th

You may be drawn back towards the past now, perhaps because you're meeting up with people from your childhood or family members you haven't seen for a long time. It's an ideal day to honour the past and let go of any regrets as you take a step into Libra season.

Monday 25th

Your mind is at its most inspirational right now, so focus on communication and learning. You may be diving deep into matters of the soul or retracing your family tree. If you're a particularly spiritual person, this is your time.

Tuesday 26th

It might be wise to intervene in someone else's life today. Use your mediating skills to ensure that a lover or friend isn't getting into bad company. This is a chance for your helpful nature to shine through.

Wednesday 27th

It may be that once a month you have a job, chore or cleaning project that you don't enjoy. If there's something you know you've been putting off, today would be a great day to tackle it. It might be boring, but at least you'll get it done.

Thursday 28th

It's not the best day for communication, either at work or at home, as you might find it hard to understand what someone else is trying to say. Instead, be patient and find ways to make life easier for both of you.

Friday 29th

Cast your mind back to events in July concerning one of your friends or a group in which you're involved. If there was a specific issue, a similar problem could arise today. If you're paying for anything online today, double-check that everything goes through automatically.

Saturday 30th

You might waste time today chasing up a payment or financial issue that's not been sorted out. It may take two or three attempts to get things sorted, but be persistent. There's a chance that an argument could get out of hand, so choose your companions carefully.

OCTOBER

. . . .

Sunday 1st

Pay close attention to money matters now and over the next month. A financial situation may be coming to an end, so ensure that you're paid what's rightfully yours. Consider getting financial or legal advice if necessary.

Monday 2nd

Someone may be trying to withhold the whole truth from you. Ensure that you aren't too trusting and try to get to the bottom of things. Read between the lines and find out what's being hidden from you.

Tuesday 3rd

If you're fed up with being lied to or disrespected, it's time to put a stop to things. You're probably not the greatest fan of conflict, but being honest doesn't necessarily have to trigger an argument. Speak your mind and persuade a member of your family to do the same.

Wednesday 4th

There's an international theme to your stars today, whether you're catching up with someone who lives abroad or planning your next holiday. If you're a linguist, your skills and talents may be in demand close to home. It's a good day to find out more about what's happening in the world.

Thursday 5th

Communication planet Mercury enters your star sign today. This is the start of a promising period for negotiation and mediation. It's the ideal moment to spend more one-to-one time with the people in your life.

Friday 6th

If there's someone you don't see eye to eye with at work, it's probably best to agree to disagree today. Accept that you have a different way of working and try not to let this come between you. Believe in yourself and ensure you're being paid what you deserve.

Saturday 7th

You might take your work home with you this weekend, or perhaps you're busy working on a new creative project. Your partner or a family member might be cross if you don't have time for them, but you need to do what's right for you. It might be best to put your work before your relationships.

Sunday 8th

There could be an argument between the ones you love today, or you might have an unpleasant run-in with an ex. Stay away from anyone who has angry vibes and don't feel that you have to put up with bad behaviour. Be around friends who know how to enjoy themselves.

Monday 9th

If you're currently feeling a lot of pressure, handle what you can without overcompensating or taking on too much. Venus moves into Virgo today, and this is your cue to rest and retreat. You may be feeling angry with yourself. If so, do your best to express yourself assertively.

Tuesday 10th

There could be a situation at work that's challenging or an argument that throws you off balance. Keep being kind and caring, but don't allow yourself to be bullied. Steer clear of angry individuals in your life and try not to let your mood dip because of the behaviour of others.

Wednesday 11th

Any tensions at home or within your family could erupt today. This will be a testing time, so you may have to dig deep to deal with a crisis. Be aware that you don't have to handle everything by yourself: encourage other people to pitch in and do their bit to help.

Thursday 12th

Action planet Mars enters Scorpio and your money zone today. This is great for getting things moving. Mars is the planet of speed and determination, so take this energy into your daily life and let it drive you.

Friday 13th

'Where there's a will, there's a way' would be a good motto for your stars today. You might have to dig deep at work, especially if you're trying to complete a deadline or dealing with a major project. It's worth working hard today.

Saturday 14th

Today's solar eclipse takes place in your star sign, and this could signify a major turning point. It's vital that you listen carefully to your instincts over the next couple of weeks. The direction you're heading in could change completely once the eclipse energy has been and gone.

Sunday 15th

This is a powerful time of transformation that might involve your wellbeing or your goals and ambitions. Either way, get ready for an exciting new beginning that emerges from a challenging time. Flex your ambitious muscle.

Monday 16th

Look out for new opportunities that come your way this week and make the most of them. There could be good news that benefits you financially, perhaps involving a gift, an inheritance or a return on an investment. Try to be bold and courageous. Expand your life.

Tuesday 17th

Believe in yourself now and ensure you're fully aware of your self-worth. As a Libra, you can sometimes listen too much to what other people have to say rather than asserting your independence. Refuse to listen to negative feedback and learn to trust yourself.

. . . .

Wednesday 18th

While there's a part of you that wants to be liked, you can't always go out of your way to please other people. If there's a situation in your life where you've been playing the role of victim, now's the time to knock it on the head.

Thursday 19th

Be wary of getting involved in conversations at work that lead nowhere and take up too much of your time. You have a lot to offer others, and this may become evident to you now. When you start talking, other people should take notice.

Friday 20th

You should feel more energised and invigorated as your self-confidence gets a boost today. You might be thinking about your appearance, or you may feel ready to redesign your image, launch a website or start a new chapter in your life. If so, you're in tune with your stars.

Saturday 21st

Today's astrology looks argumentative, so issues may arise at home or within your family. This would be a good time to take yourself out of the home and away from any problems. Be wary of a relationship that drains you and avoid any communication that has the potential to be damaging.

Sunday 22nd

Communication planet Mercury moves into your money zone today. It's important to talk about finances with the people who matter, but this isn't only about money: it's also about how you value yourself and how other people see you.

Monday 23rd

The Sun's move into Scorpio today means that now is the time to channel your energy and focus. More importantly, it's time to take responsibility for your money and earnings. Step into your power and stand up for yourself if you need to.

Tuesday 24th

You'll feel more secure at work when you have an agreement in writing. This is a good time to make sure you're not being underpaid. It might be necessary to abandon pleasantries to ensure your needs are met.

Wednesday 25th

It's sometimes best to say nothing and stay in the background, and this approach could benefit you at work today. If someone's looking for a scapegoat, don't stir the pot. Remember to be savvy about your financial situation.

Thursday 26th

It's worth making sure that you have the right people on your side over the next couple of days. This might be an adviser, an expert or someone who can do a job that you can't. Learning to delegate and outsource when necessary will save you both time and money.

Friday 27th

Consider where in life you can take a step back and let someone else take the lead. There may be a lot of pressure on you now, but that doesn't mean you have to do everything. If you're typical of your star sign, you'll know that the right partnership can be a big help.

. . . .

Saturday 28th

Today's lunar eclipse lights up your money zone. A payment plan or debt may come to an end, or a situation that's tied you up over the last couple of years could begin to ease. Keep working away to achieve your dreams, even if you have to leave other people out of the equation.

Sunday 29th

Emotions often run high during eclipse season. If you and someone close don't see eye to eye when it comes to money, this may not be the best time to start an important conversation. Tempers might flare and a difference of opinion could push you and someone close further apart.

Monday 30th

It's a good idea to consider your financial situation carefully before taking action. Security is likely to be important to you right now, both financially and emotionally. If you're currently undergoing a period of change regarding finances, you might experience some worry or instability. Don't keep your emotions bottled in.

Tuesday 31st

This is a promising time to discover more about money, so look to learn important lessons about responsibility and how much value you put on earnings and possessions. The more you know about your finances, the better.

NOVEMBER

· · · · · · · · · · · · · · · · ·

Wednesday 1st

You may feel overwhelmed by an influx of information and ideas today. Try to discern what's important and head in the right direction. This could be particularly relevant regarding a travel or study option. When it comes to work, get back in touch with your ambition.

Thursday 2nd

Different threads could come together today and help you make steady progress at work or with an important issue. Do what you can to ensure your self-belief remains strong, as this will help you to develop a more abundant mindset.

Friday 3rd

The more you know about your finances, the easier it is to make wise decisions. Making smart choices now will help you out in the year ahead. Be knowledgeable about money rather than feeling scared by it.

Saturday 4th

You could feel unsettled if a job's come to an end or you're worried about a personal issue. Try not to let fear and doubt kick in, and don't do anything rash in response to recent events. Your best move today is to hang out with your friends and forget the big decisions for a while.

Sunday 5th

It's not going to help going over and over the same issues today. You may end up arguing with a good friend or feel generally out of sorts. What you require is a welcome diversion from the trickier issues. A group event should tick all the boxes.

Monday 6th

Team up with people at home or within your wider family and pool your resources. Ensure you get paid what you deserve when it comes to your work, skills and talents. It's a good day to be persistent by going all out to get what you want. Don't let shyness stop you from getting ahead.

Tuesday 7th

When it comes to your work, use your connections to boost your prospects. Spread your net wide and don't rely solely on your current contacts. It's not a good idea to put all your eggs in one basket today. Instead, keep your options open, explore different ideas and try something new.

Wednesday 8th

Your planet Venus enters your star sign today. This is a reminder that you're at your happiest when life is balanced and harmonious. You're going to have opportunities to use your charm over the next few weeks, and doing so could help boost your popularity and good fortune. Embrace life fully.

Thursday 9th

When your relationships are out of sorts, you can feel out of sorts too. Today is a good day for getting back on track with someone close and ensuring that you're reading from the same page. Make a loving gesture and reach out to other people.

Friday 10th

Talk planet Mercury enters your communication zone today. This isn't a good time to be alone. Instead, you're being pulled out into the world and will feel urged to connect with others, either for social reasons or for more practical matters. If you're feeling lonely, reach out and engage with other people.

Saturday 11th

There's some tricky astrology today involving your partner planet Mars. You could fall out with someone close, especially if they're behaving foolishly or recklessly. Try not to get too angry or be overly impulsive and take a step back if necessary.

Sunday 12th

You have a generous nature and a charitable side to your personality. If you're typical of your star sign, your first response is probably to help other people. Today's stars indicate that you should try to support the people around you. Work with someone to come up with a joint solution.

Monday 13th

Today's new moon takes place in your finance zone. It's a good day to set your intentions around money and look for a new opportunity to earn more. However, it might be impossible to keep a tight hold of your money, especially if an unexpected expense crops up. You may have to respond fast.

Tuesday 14th

If you keep getting turned down for a promotion at work or you miss out on company benefits, it might be a good idea to try a new approach. Widen your social circle while also exploring opportunities closer to home. Get involved in your local neighbourhood or a community event.

Wednesday 15th

If you're involved in any kind of negotiation or power game, don't charge in all guns blazing. Your best bet is to be charming, so try to negotiate carefully and smooth things over. This may be particularly pertinent if it concerns a family relationship or a situation with a neighbour.

Thursday 16th

Money remains an important issue in your life. Work alongside your family by teaming up and tackling the problem. Be open and receptive to a surprising gift. Seek expert advice if you feel that it would help a situation.

Friday 17th

If you're a typical Libra, you probably have a good understanding of the give and take of life. Your community spirit is often self-evident, especially at work and within your neighbourhood. This would be a fantastic time to organise a charity event or a fund-raising initiative.

Saturday 18th

There's a lot of power in your stars today, so you should consider going all out to raise money or earn funds for a big adventure or exciting project. Persuade your family members to join in with a good cause.

Sunday 19th

You might be teaching someone about the ways of society today. Think about trying to get them involved in a humanitarian or environmental project. Pass on what you know in a fun way: learning doesn't always have to be hard.

Monday 20th

If you've been supporting other people a lot recently, it's time to look at other ways of helping. Engage your heart and goodwill to find new solutions. There's a finality about events this week, so aim to bring a project to completion.

Tuesday 21st

Be the first to show willingness at work, as doing so could benefit you in the future. The more you give, the more you may receive in return. You're likely to favour a workplace that's supportive and friendly, rather than a hard-nosed competitive environment. Be aware of this and make choices accordingly.

Wednesday 22nd

Push hard to resolve a significant issue. You will likely have extra resilience and willpower to meet a deadline or finalise an agreement today. It might be tough, but you will be glad when things are settled. Communicate well and be resilient.

Thursday 23rd

The Sun's move into Sagittarius lights up your social life, highlighting communication, friends and community. If your work or daily routine doesn't provide you with these key ingredients, it might be time to seek inspiration elsewhere. Make the most of life close to home.

Friday 24th

You may have a lot going on locally and feel that you need your fair share of fun and laughter. Ensure you have good friends on your side and people you can talk to. Over the next few weeks, you might have the chance to become more involved within your community. Gather new ideas and information.

Saturday 25th

If you're a typical Libra, your friends are important to you, and you don't like to fall out with people. However, it might be time to veer away from a challenging friendship and to look for support elsewhere. This is an excellent weekend to make a new to-do list and get yourself organised, so write down your ideas.

Sunday 26th

Don't fight your feelings today. If journalling and talking things through with your friends doesn't seem to be helping, reach out to someone who has expertise in the right area. An older relative could be the perfect sounding board for you to explore your fears and doubts.

Monday 27th

Today's full moon cuts across the areas of your horoscope linked to study, education, travel and communication. This means that you might be thinking about going back to school or gaining new qualifications, or you may realise that you want to make some new friends.

Tuesday 28th

It's a good day for being proactive and channelling your energy into a new project or an exciting adventure. If you're seeking a holiday romance or a second honeymoon, get the ball rolling. Your enthusiasm may wane later on, but that doesn't mean you're on the wrong track.

Wednesday 29th

Make an extra effort to show willingness at work and impress a person of influence. This is also an excellent time to pursue a new entrepreneurial venture. Self-belief will prove to be the key, so forge ahead with courage.

Thursday 30th

This could be a good day for taking a risk. If you're ready to start a part-time business or seeking a fulfilling vocation, here's your opportunity. Use the internet and social media to your advantage and find out which ideas interest other people.

DECEMBER

· · · · · · · · · · · · · · · · · ·

Friday 1st
Talk planet Mercury moves into your home and family zone today, so it's a good weekend to discuss what's happening in these key areas. You might find yourself making arrangements for the festive season or deciding what to do regarding someone younger in the family.

Saturday 2nd
There's a serious edge to family communications now and over the next few weeks. Don't avoid having an important conversation that could make a huge difference to someone's life. It may take a while to sort things out properly, but you should start as you mean to go on.

Sunday 3rd
Family relations matter a lot right now, even if they're not always easy to maintain. If you have a tough relationship with a family member, an old issue could flare up again today. You don't always have to put up with things: remove yourself from the situation if necessary.

Monday 4th
Your planet Venus changes star sign today and enters your money zone, where it will remain until the end of December. This is a good time to draw up a plan and work out finances and spending, especially in the run-up to the Christmas period. It may be up to you to take charge.

Tuesday 5th

As a Libra, you're likely to be one of life's givers. However, it's important to prioritise your own interests right now, especially regarding money. You might want to treat the ones you love, but make sure you keep an eye on your finances.

Wednesday 6th

You might feel sentimental today, especially if you hear a sad story at work. You may find that you shed a tear at the drop of a hat, especially at a time when your compassionate nature is boundless and your heart is open and sensitive. Offer your services to a person in need this evening.

Thursday 7th

The moon graces your star sign today, so it's a great opportunity to turn on your signature charm and use your persuasive abilities to make big strides towards a personal goal. You might be able to connect with people close to home or in your community who can help you develop your plans or aims further, so reach out.

Friday 8th

Lucky Jupiter is in action today, and this could spell good news for you, especially if a family member offers to help you out. You may want to think about trying to earn extra money. If you dig around, you may find a hidden treasure.

Saturday 9th

If you're helping out at a school fair or a community Christmas event, things could go extremely well this weekend. This may also be true if you run an art business or you're selling your wares at the market or a car boot sale. Use your communication skills to bring in the punters.

Sunday 10th

Today is a good day to make a difference in the world, perhaps by supporting a local business or deciding to shop more sustainably. You could also consider volunteering or giving up your time to help others. Sharing your energy with the world can only improve how you feel.

Monday 11th

It's a good day for all forms of communication. This includes talking through plans with your family, teaching a local class or learning something new. When you're actively engaged with the world, you receive so many additional benefits that you may not have even considered.

Tuesday 12th

Today's new moon highlights your communication zone, and is about your social life, having fun and making connections. This is an opportunity to wipe the slate clean and start over, so reach out to other people.

Wednesday 13th

Communication planet Mercury turns retrograde in your home and family zone today, so slow down the pace. It might be best to put off any major home or family-related decisions until early January. Give yourself time and space to think about new developments related to your personal affairs.

Thursday 14th

If someone's offered to help you out, there may be a delay, or perhaps they've changed their mind. This doesn't mean it's not going to happen, but you might have to be patient. When it comes to a major decision, it might be best to wait until 2024 before committing.

Friday 15th

You won't be pleased if someone close has gone back on their word, but they may have a good reason for doing so. Rather than cutting someone off completely, consider your emotional response and try to understand what triggers this reaction.

Saturday 16th

It's a wonderful weekend to get involved in a big family get-together. Being around people you love will help to lift your spirits and remind you of the innocence of life. A passionate encounter could be on the cards this evening.

Sunday 17th

You'll be happiest today when you're being sociable or joining in with a community event. A music festival or concert may arouse your emotions and transport you back into the past. Try not to worry about work, even if you know you've got a lot to do before the end of the year.

Monday 18th

It's worth reopening a conversation today. You can't expect an immediate solution when it comes to a home or family issue, but you can still remind someone that you're there if they need you. Someone from your past could reappear in your life and may bring a gift or blessing you weren't expecting.

Tuesday 19th

It won't be easy to concentrate if you're at work today, so don't line up a heavy schedule. You might be enjoying a boozy Christmas lunch or be involved with festive plans in the office. If you're in a relationship, it's worth waiting up late to spend time with the one you love.

Wednesday 20th

It's a good day for a heart-to-heart with someone special. If frustrations or niggles have been increasing between you recently, have a conversation about them, as this could stop them from turning into a major issue. Even if you're saying the same thing over and over again, be persistent.

Thursday 21st

You may experience a change to your income, expenses or outgoings today. This isn't a great day to act impulsively, especially when it comes to love. If there's a falling out, try to smooth things over as best you can, at work and at home.

Friday 22nd

Remember that it's the season of goodwill, so it's best to put any recent disappointments behind you and get involved with festivities close to home. You might be lucky today and win a raffle, or perhaps a conversation with a family member this evening proves to be a significant turning point.

Saturday 23rd

Talk planet Mercury retreats into your communication zone today. This is often a time when you hear from someone from your past, perhaps in the form of a letter or Christmas card in the post. Don't get hung up on buying expensive presents, and instead offer gifts of love and help.

Sunday 24th

There's a multicultural feel to your stars today, so your heart may be with someone who's abroad this Christmas, or you might feel closely connected to people from a different culture. This evening, choose to put duty and responsibility first and visit an elderly relative or spend quality time with your family.

Monday 25th

If you're enjoying a holiday abroad this Christmas, you're in tune with your stars. Wherever you are, there's plenty to be happy about. Your planet Venus is in pole position right now, and this means that you'll be at the centre of things. One of your gifts could make a huge difference.

Tuesday 26th

Try not to get involved in an argument today, as any difference of opinion will be difficult to overcome. If you know someone in your family has opposing views to you, keep quiet. This evening, turn your attention to the coming year and think about what you want for yourself and your family.

Wednesday 27th

Today's full moon highlights your past and your future. Spend time talking to your family, hear their thoughts and ask for advice and support yourself. Being around family or people close to you should leave you feeling loved and secure. Create a safe base for yourself and the ones you love.

Thursday 28th

Some conversations could be awkward now, especially if they reveal where you and your loved ones differ when it comes to morals and ethics. If you're a typical Libra, you care about everyone and you dislike bigotry and prejudice. Choose what you say and who you hang out with carefully.

Friday 29th

It could be a busy end of the year for you, whether you're working in a lively environment, checking in on the neighbours or joining in with a community venture. Team up with other people and work towards a good cause. It's time to get back out into the world.

Saturday 30th

Widen your social circle and be around like-minded people as the year comes to a close. Your friends matter a lot to you, and meeting new people could spark new ideas or excitement as 2023 winds down. Join in with a social event that guarantees fun and laughter this evening.

Sunday 31st

If you feel a heart-to-heart would benefit a family member or someone you live with, now's the time to speak up. If you want to create an environment in which you can help each other out, here's your opportunity. Be with the ones you love.

Libra

....

PEOPLE WHO SHARE
YOUR SIGN

PEOPLE WHO SHARE YOUR SIGN

· · · · · · · · · · · · · · · · · ·

For decades, Librans have been the zodiac's providers of balance and beauty. From famous lawyers such as Judge Judy to fashion designers such as Ralph Lauren, Librans can be fair and fashionable. Whether they blow fans away with their talents or raise friends up with their positive energy, they are sure to charm themselves into the hearts of many. Discover the Librans who share your birthday and see if you can spot the similarities.

24th September
Ben Platt (1993), Pia Wurtzbach (1989), Kimberley Nixon (1985), Stephanie McMahon (1976), Jackie Sandler (1974), Kevin Sorbo (1958), Phil Hartman (1948), Jim Henson (1936), F. Scott Fitzgerald (1896)

25th September
Donald Glover (1983), Declan Donnelly (1975), Catherine Zeta-Jones (1969), Will Smith (1968), Keely Shaye Smith (1963), Heather Locklear (1961), Michael Madsen (1957), Christopher Reeve (1952), Mark Hamill (1951), Michael Douglas (1944), William Faulkner (1897)

26th September
Talulah Riley (1985), Nev Schulman (1984), Jon Richardson (1982), Christina Milian (1981), Serena Williams (1981), Petro Poroshenko, Ukrainian President (1965), Olivia Newton-John (1948), T. S. Eliot (1888)

27th September

Simona Halep (1991), Lola Kirke (1990), Avril Lavigne (1984), Anna Camp (1982), Lil Wayne (1982), Carrie Brownstein (1974), Gwyneth Paltrow (1972), Marc Maron (1963)

28th September

Hilary Duff (1987), St. Vincent (1982), Bam Margera (1979), Naomi Watts (1968), Mira Sorvino (1967), Brigitte Bardot (1934), Bhagat Singh (1907)

29th September

Halsey (1994), Kevin Durant (1988), Dani Pedrosa (1985), Zachary Levi (1980), Roger Bart (1962), Ian McShane (1942), Jerry Lee Lewis (1935)

30th September

Levi Miller (2002), Maddie Ziegler (2002), Max Verstappen (1997), Olivier Giroud (1986), Lacey Chabert (1982), Kieran Culkin (1982), Marion Cotillard (1975), Monica Bellucci (1964)

1st October

Brie Larson (1989), Matthew Daddario (1987), Sarah Drew (1980), Zach Galifianakis (1969), Theresa May (1956), André Rieu (1949), Julie Andrews (1935), George Peppard (1928), Jimmy Carter, U.S. President (1924)

2nd October

Camilla Belle (1986), Kelly Ripa (1970), Lorraine Bracco (1954), Sting (1951), Annie Leibovitz (1949), Donna Karan (1948), Don McLean (1945), Johnnie Cochran (1937), Groucho Marx (1890), Mahatma Gandhi (1869)

3rd October

Alicia Vikander (1988), Ashlee Simpson (1984), Tessa Thompson (1983), Seann William Scott (1976), Neve Campbell (1973), Lena Headey (1973), Gwen Stefani (1969), Clive Owen (1964), Al Sharpton (1954), Yohji Yamamoto (1943)

4th October

Dakota Johnson (1989), Stacey Solomon (1989), Melissa Benoist (1988), Caitriona Balfe (1979), Alicia Silverstone (1976), Liev Schreiber (1967), Christoph Waltz (1956), Susan Sarandon (1946), Charlton Heston (1923)

5th October

Jacob Tremblay (2006), Nicola Roberts (1985), Jesse Eisenberg (1983), Nicky Hilton (1983), Kate Winslet (1975), Guy Pearce (1967), Bernie Mac (1957), Imran Khan, Pakistani Prime Minister (1952), Bob Geldof (1951)

6th October

Jazz Jennings (2000), Olivia Thirlby (1986), Jeremy Sisto (1974), Ioan Gruffudd (1973), Romero Britto (1963), Elisabeth Shue (1963), Britt Ekland (1942), Jerry Heller (1940)

7th October

Kira Kosarin (1997), Diego Costa (1988), Holland Roden (1986), Alesha Dixon (1978), Thom Yorke (1968), Toni Braxton (1967), Simon Cowell (1959)

8th October

Bella Thorne (1997), Barbara Palvin (1993), Bruno Mars (1985), Travis Pastrana (1983), Nick Cannon (1980), Matt Damon (1970), Anne-Marie Duff (1970), Sigourney Weaver (1949), Chevy Chase (1943), R.L. Stine (1943), Jesse Jackson (1941), Paul Hogan (1939)

9th October

Bella Hadid (1996), Tyler James Williams (1992), Chris O'Dowd (1979), Brandon Routh (1979), David Cameron (1966), Scott Bakula (1954), Sharon Osbourne (1952), Jackson Browne (1948), John Lennon (1940)

10th October

Xherdan Shaqiri (1991), Marina Diamandis (1985), Dan Stevens (1982), Mario Lopez (1973), Wendi McLendon-Covey (1969), Tanya Tucker (1958), David Lee Roth (1954), Nora Roberts (1950), Charles Dance (1946)

11th October

Michelle Trachtenberg (1985), Bradley James (1983), Matt Bomer (1977), Emily Deschanel (1976), Jane Krakowski (1968), Luke Perry (1966), Joan Cusack (1962), Dawn French (1957), Fred Trump (1905), Eleanor Roosevelt (1884)

12th October

Josh Hutcherson (1992), Calum Scott (1988), Tyler Blackburn (1986), Katie Piper (1983), Hugh Jackman (1968), Hiroyuki Sanada (1960), Luciano Pavarotti (1935)

13th October

Tiffany Trump (1993), Ashanti (1980), David Haye (1980), Sacha Baron Cohen (1971), Kate Walsh (1967), Kelly Preston (1962), Beverly Johnson (1952), Paul Simon (1941), Margaret Thatcher (1925)

14th October

Rowan Blanchard (2001), Lourdes Leon (1996), Usher (1978), Natalie Maines (1974), Steve Coogan (1965), Cliff Richard (1940), Ralph Lauren (1939), Roger Moore (1927), E. E. Cummings (1894), Dwight D. Eisenhower, U.S. President (1890)

15th October

Anthony Joshua (1989), Mesut Özil (1988), Keyshia Cole (1981), Dominic West (1969), Tanya Roberts (1955), Richard Carpenter (1946), A. P. J. Abdul Kalam, Indian President (1931), Friedrich Nietzsche (1844)

16th October

Naomi Osaka (1997), John Mayer (1977), Davina McCall (1967), Flea (1962), Tim Robbins (1958), Angry Grandpa (1950), Angela Lansbury (1925), Oscar Wilde (1854)

17th October

Felicity Jones (1983), Kimi Räikkönen (1979), Matthew Macfadyen (1974), Eminem (1972), Ziggy Marley (1968), Evel Knievel (1938), Rita Hayworth (1918), Arthur Miller (1915)

18th October

Tyler Posey (1991), Zac Efron (1987), Freida Pinto (1984),
Ne-Yo (1979), Jean-Claude Van Damme (1960), Martina
Navratilova (1956), Chuck Berry (1926), Pierre Trudeau,
Canadian Prime Minister (1919)

19th October

Hunter King (1993), Rebecca Ferguson (1983), Gillian Jacobs
(1982), Desmond Harrington (1976), Trey Parker (1969), Jon
Favreau (1966), John Lithgow (1945), Michael Gambon (1940)

20th October

Jess Glynne (1989), Candice Swanepoel (1988), John Krasinski
(1979), Snoop Dogg (1971), Dannii Minogue (1971), Si King
(1966), Viggo Mortensen (1958), Danny Boyle (1956), James
Chadwick (1891)

21st October

Glen Powell (1988), Amber Rose (1983), Kim Kardashian
(1980), Andrew Scott (1976), Ken Watanabe (1959), Carrie
Fisher (1956), Patti Davis (1952), Judy Sheindlin "Judge Judy"
(1942), Alfred Nobel (1833)

22nd October

Corey Hawkins (1988), Deontay Wilder (1985), Spike Jonze
(1969), Shaggy (1968), Bob Odenkirk (1962), Jeff Goldblum
(1952), Arsène Wenger (1949), Deepak Chopra (1946),
Christopher Lloyd (1938), Franz Liszt (1811)

23rd October

Amandla Stenberg (1998), Ireland Baldwin (1995), Jessica Stroup (1986), Izabel Goulart (1984), Cat Deeley (1976), Ryan Reynolds (1976), "Weird Al" Yankovic (1959), Martin Luther King III (1957), Ang Lee (1954), Pelé (1940)